# LEWI PETHRUS

# LEWI PETHRUS

## A Spiritual Memoir

LOGOS INTERNATIONAL
Plainfield, New Jersey

International Standard Book Number: 0-88270-043-X
Library of Congress Catalog Card Number: 73-75956
©Copyright 1973 Logos International, Plainfield, N.J. 07060
Printed in the United States of America

# CONTENTS

# Introduction

My baptism in the Holy Spirit occurred with miraculous results in 1902 and was followed just five years later by the beginning of the Pentecostal revival in Sweden.

Such a long firsthand experience has created in me a strong desire to delve beyond the merely outward manifestations and lay bare the most decisive factors in the birth and continued development of the modern Pentecostal movement. An exhaustive study of the Bible on Pentecostalism and fellowship with Spirit-filled believers around the world have also created a faith that craves expression.

# Foreword

Many extensive scientific studies of the Pentecostal movement have been undertaken and large volumes have been written, with varying results. In Sweden, university professors like Emanuel Linderhold, Efraim Briem, and Hjalmar Sunden have made studies in depth. In the neighboring countries of Norway, Denmark, and Finland many books have also been written on the subject.

Much of what has been said has been positive and has thrown light upon certain religio-historical problems. This can especially be said about Hjalmar Sunden's work, *Religion Och Rolleria (Religion and the Roles)*.

It is apparent, however, that the one who personally experiences what the scientists only theoretically treat should know more about it than those who view it from a distance. This judgment must be valid, even though the one with personal experience may not have at his disposal the scientific apparatus available to the scholar.

I see before me the image of these historians and religio-psychologists viewing the Pentecostal movement as a religious and sociological phenomenon. They stand on a lookout point before an expansive landscape, and their task is to give an account of the area in view. Their material is made up of what they have read about this territory and of what they have learned from persons who live within the area. Among them, however, is a man who has read most of what has been written about this countryside, who has mingled with thousands of the most informed connoisseurs of the area, and who owns source material and records. Besides this, he has a qualification that must be considered most important: he has traversed the area in every direction during a long lifetime.

Like the rest of them at that lookout point, this latter person gazes out over the panorama, but he sees more than the ridges and is not dependent on his imagination for what the valleys may look like. He has personally, inch by inch, covered the roads down in the valleys of deepest humiliation and often with great effort climbed up the steep hills. He has also been refreshed by the flowing brooks, and on the mountaintops he has rejoiced over all the beautiful, good and useful experiences he has had during the long journey.

We should be grateful for those who have called to the attention of scientists the spiritual phenomena of the Pentecostal experience. The religio-psychological area and, by and large, the soul-life of man have been the objects of very little investigation in Sweden. And the value of such research is limited. Like most scientific inquiries, it is dependent on secondhand knowledge. Such knowledge is not enough for a testimony in a court of law, a testimony that would lead to a final court ruling. This demands a testimony of what the witness personally has heard, seen, and experienced.

Having lived through one of church history's most interesting and remarkable eras, I desire to testify to what I have seen, heard, and experienced and point to the sources of life and power behind all this. During some months of quietness I have had opportunity to settle down and survey the wide fields of spiritual experience I have lived through.

I am deeply aware of how easy it is to become subjective when one speaks of events where one personally played an important role. With a serious effort to be objective and truthful, however, this will be an account of what one among many has experienced in the greatest contemporary spiritual revival.

It is a glorious landscape that opens up before us — one, as I have stated, that science has not been able to map. This account can therefore be likened to an explorer's description of a territory whose map has many blank areas and those are the areas containing many and great riches.

Many times I have been asked about the success that always accompanied this movement. In retrospect I can in a factual manner discern what has happened and point out the correlation of cause and effect.

It will be my joy to share with my reader the secret of success, as I know it.

* * *

In the present state of development of this revival we are experiencing a mighty outpouring of the Spirit upon churches and denominations which earlier were untouched by this kind of spiritual life, and we see a marked awakening among multitudes who heretofore were completely foreign to a vital Christianity. No doubt, these who so recently have been introduced to the Pentecostal experience can learn some lessons from what has happened in the past.

This volume is not to be considered an infallible guide to those who lately have joined us on this wonderful path of experience. With all the blessings added to those who have learned to know the abundant power of the baptism in the Holy Spirit, many mistakes and imperfections have been brought to light. This is inevitable in everything where man has a part. This is, however, the human side. But there is present in this revival a divine side, a supernatural aspect, which we can never fully appreciate, and the depth of which we can never search.

Those who come borne by the new spiritual wave, when God pours out His Spirit upon all flesh, may not in all respects be able to follow the way of previous revivals, but they can, no doubt, find various things in the life and ministry of the spiritual predecessors which can be very helpful. The mistakes made by past spiritual movements may be especially important to apprehend.

It is of great value to the mariner sailing in strange waters that those who went before charted the course and marked the unseen shoals. If a similar procedure is followed in our realm of concern, a spiritual movement can become purer and sounder with the passing of time.

The outpouring of the Spirit, which now is attracting the attention of the whole world, and which in some areas is known as the charismatic renewal, is nothing new. It is a continuation of the movement which began on the first day of Pentecost in Jerusalem and which since then has been repeated over and over throughout history and in this century has been known as the Pentecostal movement.

It is of little or no significance that there are differences of fields of ministry, expressions and forms. God meets man where he is, makes him more natural than ever, and uses him the way he is. It is important that we realize this concerning various Christian fields of labor so that we do not demand uniformity of one another. Every evidence of a generation gap among the people of this revival must be banned. No people have as great possibilities to be "of one heart and of one soul" as those who experience the baptism in the Holy Spirit and are led by the Holy Spirit.

Against the background sketched above and with the indicated convictions, the author is following a definite prompting of the Spirit to make this contribution to our rich contemporary literature concerning the outpouring of the Spirit in the last days.

# The Individual Surrender

My own experience

## THE DECISION OF THE INDIVIDUAL

We speak much about various collectives in reference to the work of God in the world, but basically this work is built entirely upon the individual. It is through individual people that God is working, and this applies not only to the leaders but to everyone who is a part of the Christian fellowship.

St. Augustine said that the church was holy even if the members were not. But there is no such abstract church apart from the members. As is the individual member, so is the church.

Therefore it is very interesting and instructive to study God's way with the individual. He leads different people in different ways, but there are some experiences which we must share alike. We must have a personal meeting with God and be restored to fellowship with Him. This is a very personal volitional act, when through a personal decision one surrenders his life to God. In this respect the collective, such as a big revival service, gives a superficial and misguiding impression. If there be thousands who simultaneously indicate that they seek God, it is nevertheless upon the individual decision that the real experience depends. It is the individual in the large group who has a personal experience and surrenders to God. And the cause of the local church as well as Christianity at large depends upon the decision and the continued spiritual life of the individual.

The experience of the individual is therefore of

tremendous importance. Many have had the same experience as this author, and he is familiar with many of them, but he knows no experience better than his own. Therefore, desiring to share such a personal experience with his readers, he will give some glimpses from his own spiritual emergence.

## DESIRE FOR GOD

From my early youth I have been conscious of a clearly drawn aim: it has been a seeking for blessing upon my life but not for selfish purposes. My desire has been for blessing to rest upon my calling in life. Success has been sought not for myself nor for selfish, material gains. My striving has not been for a position but for the privilege of being useful in the environment where I have been placed.

Early in life I had a premonition of my future mission. It was a very insignificant incident which brought this timid latent feeling to light. I would never have thought of claiming a divine call to be a preacher. One day, however, not long after I had been baptized in water, I was on my way to work in company with Varner Hogberg, the father of Daniel Berg (who later became known as one of the earliest Pentecostal missionaries to Brazil). He spoke to me about the step I had taken in that I had been baptized and become a member of the church. During the course of our conversation he said: "If you remain faithful to the Lord and live for Him I believe you will be a preacher some day."

This came as a total surprise to me, and as far as I can recall I didn't answer him. It was, however, a remarkable experience to have someone else remark about a feeling I so timidly had kept in my own heart and mind. The effect of this upon me was like that of a seed which for some time has been sprouting in the ground, and then suddenly the first tender blade pushes through the crust of the earth. That which is hidden in darkness comes to light and for the first time enjoys the warm and life-giving rays of the sun. From that day my awareness of a divine call was a reality for me, and from that time this call dominated to a great extent my life, although I was only 15 at the time.

Shortly after this experience I moved from my parents' home which had been a quiet corner where my sensitive mind had had the stillness and quietness it needed at the crisis which precipitated full assurance of salvation and an open confession of my Christian faith.

There I had the support of dad and mother for my growing life of faith, and there I had the forest just steps outside the door where I spent much time during the summers; and there I had found a meeting place with God.

At that time my desire for God increased, and I longed to experience more of the things I believed in. No doubt, every new convert, and not least the alert youths, have this hunger and thirst for spiritual realities. How often they go with their longing for God, but without guidance!

My home was out in the country, at the foot of a mountain called Hallegerg, located about six miles from the city of Vanersborg in Vastergotland, Sweden. I was employed by A.F. Karlson's Shoe Factory in Vanersborg, where I was working amongst hundreds of fellows. Daily I had to answer questions regarding the Bible and my Christian faith.

This meant a great deal for the development of my spiritual life. Both my life and profession as a Christian had been spotlighted, and I had to maintain the position I had taken from the beginning. The move from my home, however, probably meant even more to my desire for more of God.

In my new living quarters I shared a room with two young men, but both of them were much older than I. Although kind and personable men, they were not Christians. One of them used liquor and was sometimes quite intoxicated. The other one was a total abstainer. Both of them played cards, and this seemed to occupy most of their time in our room.

In this kind of environment, something altogether strange to me, I had to live as a Christian. I had come from my home where I had been surrounded by godly fear and prayer. In this new environment, however, I had a deep longing in my heart to live for God, although I felt my spiritual weakness under these conditions. If I were to remain a dedicated Christian and confess the name of Jesus around me I had to have a richer experience of the power of God. This was an awareness which developed into a crying need.

At that time the Salvation Army had come to Vanersborg. This was something new for our community, and people around me talked about their meetings. Some officer from their ranks who had visited the city had spoken about the baptism in the Holy Spirit. This also was something altogether new which I had never before heard anything about; now I heard of it from one of the fellows at work. Thus I was led to read the Bible, where in the Book of Acts I saw how the first Christians had a definite experience which the Scriptures call being baptized in the Holy Spirit. My concept of this was still very cloudy, but on the other hand I knew very clearly that I needed more power to be a true Christian in my everyday life.

The very first night I moved into my quarters in the city I had a very strong awareness of this need. My two roommates occupied the table with their card playing and filled the room with the language of card players. Every night before I went to bed I had been used to reading the Bible and to kneeling in prayer. That first night I had a real struggle before I got out my New Testament which had been given to me in Sunday school. Finally, I did read a chapter while the cards were hitting the table.

My prayer time was observed as usual. Maybe the reading did not convey too much meaning to me and neither did I receive too much edification through this time of worship, but still, I had won a victory. I had professed my Christian faith before my new roommates. This and similar experiences created within me a deepening longing for spiritual power.

Thus I went to my pastor. He was a God-fearing man; about a year earlier he had baptized me in water on February 12, 1899. It may be of interest to my readers to know that I was baptized at the same time as another 15-year-old, a child-hood friend of mine. His name is Daniel Berg, and he later was to become one of the founders of the wonderful Pentecostal revival in Brazil, one of the most remarkable spiritual movements of the 20th century. Anyhow, just about a year after that baptismal service, I looked up the minister who had officiated at the time. My purpose was to speak to him about the deep longing I had for a richer life in God. In my memory I can still see the picture of that meeting so vividly. We were out in the yard of the Baptist church in Vanersborg. The pastor came from the woodshed, where he had been chopping wood, and I came from my simple lodging. I shared with him my concern and asked him if in our time also we could expect to receive the baptism in the Holy Spirit as someone had stated at the Salvation Army service.

While I had been thinking about these things, I had read the New Testament and seen that in early Christian times the believers had this experience even after they had been baptized in water. Now the minister explained to me that this was an experience which belonged to the early Christian era. Such supernatural phenomena were necessary then in order to confirm Christianity; thus the experience was not for our days. The measure of the Spirit we could expect, we received at the time of our water baptism, and then we had to live by faith and ought not to expect such supernatural things.

The disappointment I sensed at this explanation, and the spiritual impotence that I experienced, I can still recall until this day! Many thoughts occupied the mind of the sad young man who that night returned to his lodging. My pastor had my absolute confidence, but how could I understand the New Testament record? How could I understand what I read about experiences in the household of Cornelius and the twelve disciples in Ephesus? What could I do about my crying need for more power?

How happy they were, I thought, who lived in apostolic times and who could receive this wonderful power of God. Oh, if we had only had the privilege to live in a time when the promise of the Holy Spirit still was in effect!

My personal experience from my early youth has always caused me to think with sympathetic understanding of how difficult many Christians may find it to be in churches where they get no guidance and help in their often deep desire for God. Young people are much of the time described as superficial and shallow. One says that they only want superficiality and entertainment, but my observation is that when they meet spiritual reality they are more open for it than older Christians.

It causes one to tremble just to think that a young person longing for the power of God and having a very legitimate need of serving the Lord may be left without help even by his pastor. There are thousands of such young people today who, as it were, hear the purling sound of the early Christian springs of power, but their spiritual guides lead them away. What a loss for individual Christians! What a loss for the Christian church! What a loss to the world! At the same time, what a responsibility for him who makes himself available for service in this needy field!

These experiences and similar ones have convinced me that the desire for God in man is a power which will safeguard the victory of God's kingdom. Its presence in the heart of man leaves him no rest until that longing for God has been satisfied. Where we would least expect it, this thirst for God breaks through the crust like a volcano, and there is no power that can stop it. Even Christian leaders who cannot grasp or understand the work of the Spirit cannot hinder the longing for God in the individual.

Here the divine call combines with such a spiritual hunger and thirst that they create springs in an arid desert land.

The longing for God is the limitless capital upon which is based all spiritual experience, all spiritual revival, and all true success in the kingdom of God.

## THE BAPTISM IN THE HOLY SPIRIT

In 1946 a team from Youth for Christ visited

Stockholm: they were a group of young men under the leadership of Dr. Torrey Johnson from Chicago. In cooperation with the pastors from the Mission Covenant Church, the Methodist Church, and the Baptist Church I arranged meetings for them in our city. We had large meetings, and churches and auditoriums were filled to capacity even at the noonday meetings.

There were four or five young Americans who brought great blessings with the message they delivered. At the close of their visit they said to me: "Pastor Pethrus, we would very much like to have a chat with you before we leave." We engaged in that conversation one of the last days of their stay.

Sitting in their hotel lobby, one of them said to me: "Can you tell us the secret of your success in your work? Could you state it in just a few words?"

I replied: "If I were to respond in Swedish I could tell you the answer in one word — 'Andedopet' — the baptism in the Holy Spirit." Among the young Americans was Billy Graham, although this happened before he had become known all over the world.

At the World Council in Uppsala in 1968 Billy Graham was present as an observer, and he visited my home. He raised a number of questions, and the first one was: "Tell me, Brother Pethrus, do you have the same opinion today as you did many years ago concerning the baptism in the Holy Spirit and speaking in tongues?"

My response was that my conviction concerning the baptism in the Holy Spirit and its importance was the same, and if possible more confirmed than ever.

More than one has asked me this question over the years, and I have always given the same answer. The baptism in the Holy Spirit is the secret in my life as a Christian and in my ministry, and also in that of my fellow workers.

In order to get to this period of my personal experience, it will be necessary to bypass important events which led me to the baptism in the Holy Spirit. I will later bring these events into focus. The way in which God met me has become more and more interesting and more enlightening as I have continued to study questions related to this area of truth.

My experience dates back to a time when hardly anybody preached the baptism in the Holy Spirit, at least not in the circles where I was moving. It took place five years before the Pentecostal revival came to Sweden. It happened in such a way that it is absolutely excluded that there could be any such influence as the power of suggestion. This is particularly true when it comes to my speaking in tongues, for I was completely unprepared for this. I did not quite know what happened to me when under the influence of a mighty power which filled my entire being I began to speak words that I could not understand.

Neither was there any external reason compelling me to pray. Often trials and difficulties cause people to turn to God, but I had nothing of such a nature at that time. Everything was bright and wonderful, and I saw the opportunities and challenges of a young person before me. I had a good position, although at this particular time I had a leave of absence in order to go on a preaching trip. I had many friends and I was very happy with my lot in life. Really, I had only one concern at that time and that was whether I should remain in my secular employment or go into full-time Gospel work.

I have an idea that I was one of the happiest and most talkative in the circle of young men with whom I associated in the Baptist Church in Oslo, Norway. A group of young people from the Sunday school were busy with some woodcraft in the basement of the Tabernacle when the pastor of the church, Rev. Jakob Ohrn, came down to us. While talking to us about what we were doing, he eventually told us the real reason for his coming. Pastor Adolf Milde in Arendal had written and asked him to send a young man who could assist him with the work at the outstations of the church.

Now Pastor Ohrn turned to one of the older fellows, Hildor Back, who was a gifted speaker and often conducted his own services. He said that he could not go, for he had promised to accept another offer.

With a burning desire to enter that type of a ministry I heard their conversation, but the pastor did not ask me. No doubt, he considered me too young and inexperienced. Just how it all came about I cannot recall, but I was given the opportunity to go to this place. I remained at Arendal over Pentecost Sunday that year and then moved to Lillesand, a tiny harbor on the east side of the Norwegian "sorlandet" — southland.

For a couple of weeks we had meetings there, and the people showed me much love. Many came to the services, and everything was joy and gratitude. After my last Sunday services there, I was scheduled to return to Oslo; the large Bergensboat departed at 4:00 A.M. on Monday morning, and I was to leave on that boat.

While I was ministering in this little town of Lillesand, I learned to know some friends who spoke of a deeper life in God. They spoke of experiences like divine healing, which in a special way attracted my interest. One of the ladies suggested that a group of us should get together in her home after the Sunday evening service. She would serve some refreshments, and then we could share fellowship in prayer until it was time to leave for the boat on Monday morning at 4:00 A.M. I thought it was an excellent suggestion.

The couple in whose house we gathered had been to America and participated in the services conducted by Dr. Dowie in Zion City. One of the others in that circle of friends was a member of a Holiness group which at that time was quite well-known in Norway. No doubt, it was their thoughtfulness regarding the young "makings of a preacher" that caused them to arrange this meeting, and I believe this gathering was of tremendous importance in what I later experienced.

We prayed all night until it was time to leave for the boat. All of them accompanied me down to the pier. It was a beautiful morning, just at the dawn of one of the matchless pre-summer mornings of the north. I can still remember the tender love and the well-wishes of these newfound friends, and the impression of the glorious services is just as vivid. In such a frame of mind I boarded the ship.

I was the only passenger from Lillesand. I watched the sailors pull in the gangway and the boat launch out while the little blessed band of believers waved farewell.

With all of this over I remained on deck — alone. Others were sleeping in their cabins. The seamen who had taken care of the gangway disappeared, and I could continue the prayer I had been engaged in through the night. While I stood there by the railing and prayed, the sun rose up out of the ocean. I have always been impressed by the majesty and beauty of nature, but this time I experienced something altogether new. The experiences of this last night, my contact with God through prayer, and the wonderful scenery of nature before me — all seemed to overwhelm me.

Tears streamed down my cheeks while I was overflowing with joy. A current of power and sweetness went through my entire being, and I spoke strange words which surprised me a great deal. In this condition I continued to experience the power of God, and remained on deck for a long time until the boat was way out at sea before I began to settle down for the long voyage.

It was not until the Pentecostal revival broke through and Pastor Barratt came to Norway with the message about the baptism in the Spirit that I understood what I had experienced on board the ship in 1902 was the baptism in the Holy Ghost accompanied by this sign of tongues.

On another occasion I shared with a pastor my experiences in conjunction with my visit to Lillesand, but he warned me against the friends with whom I had spent the night of prayer. In his opinion they belonged to a group which proclaimed an exaggerated holiness message, and I ought to be careful of any influence from that direction.

Because I did not know any teaching concerning the baptism in the Holy Spirit, I never spoke about it, although from then on I continued to devote all my time to preaching the Gospel. The experience was, nevertheless, a strength in my spiritual life and in my ministry. I saw great results of my preaching for revival following me at all my meetings. Thus, before I came to a clear understanding of the Pentecostal message, I experienced extensive revivals in the provinces of Skane and Vastergotland in Sweden. The experience of the baptism in the Holy Spirit out on the ocean left deep and lasting impressions on my life and ministry.

Though I saw great results in conversions through my ministry, no one received the baptism in the Holy Spirit during the first five years after my experience. I just did not realize that I had experienced the baptism in the Holy Spirit; consequently, I could not preach this truth nor teach it.

"Faith cometh by hearing, and hearing by the word of God" (Rom. 10:17). Experience in itself is not enough, but we must understand the doctrine in order to be able to preach what we have experienced. Not until then will we see others receive the experience as the result of our preaching.

This experience of mine has also taught me something that I have often wondered about. We have read about God's messengers throughout the centuries who have been mighty instruments in the hands of the Lord. We have read their biographies and studied about the remarkable things they accomplished in the kingdom of God, yet, we never heard that they were baptized in the Holy Spirit. I believe, however, that these did have the baptism in the Holy Spirit. They had the experience although they never realized what it really was, and therefore, they had really little reason to speak about it and to preach about the baptism in the Holy Spirit.

When I had had this experience I never spoke about it; it seemed so wonderful and sacred that I wanted to keep it to myself. Once when I spoke to a spiritual leader about it, I was warned against super-spirituality. If the Pentecostal revival had not come my way, I would, doubtless, have passed from the earthly scene with this experience hidden in my own heart.

No doubt, many of God's instruments, men whom God has used in a marvelous way in His service, have had this experience. They were sealed by the Holy Spirit, although it was never made known when and how it happened.

## PENTECOSTAL BEGINNINGS IN 1907

My experience of the Pentecostal revival, as I was introduced to it in 1907, was an absolutely outstanding event in my life. It was a step forward for me personally in my spiritual experience. Never during the years since then has a thought entered my mind that my way through life could have been different than the one I have passed as a preacher of the apostolic Pentecostal experience.

I have earlier described my situation when the Pentecostal revival broke in on Scandinavia. Through the religious press I had read some about the revival accompanied by speaking in tongues which was reported in Los Angeles, California, U.S.A., but I had never given much thought to it. Through a bold first-page feature article in Sweden's largest newspaper, however, I learned that this revival had come to Oslo (then known as Kristiania), Norway, and that Pastor T. B. Barratt was the preacher who proclaimed these new things, and my interest became more intense. I knew Pastor Barratt and had heard him preach in Kristiania, so when I saw his name connected with the revival which was criticized in the newspaper, it gave me a great deal of confidence in the revival. Besides, much of what was stated in this report agreed with my spiritual position, so I immediately decided to go to Norway and observe this.

Within a week I had left for the Norwegian capital. My purpose was not just to study the revival, as many preachers and priests did. My desire was to partake of this new blessing which now had come. And I was not to become disappointed.

I met something new, and I still maintain this opinion that

with the Pentecostal message something new came to Christianity in particular and humanity in general. There have been treasures which have been long lost from Christian preaching, treasures which the Pentecostal message brought back to the Christian church and to its preaching.

My concept of the experience of the baptism in the Holy Spirit was of such dimensions that the experience I had had on board the ship outside the city of Lillesand near the Norwegian coast in 1902 all but vanished. I was given the impression that the baptism in the Holy Spirit with the manifestations described in the papers was something far greater than what I had experienced in my solitude. It was reported that people were smitten to the floor, that they went into ecstasy, and that when speaking in tongues, they lost all conscious control. You see, I had never seen a person receive the baptism in the Holy Spirit, neither had I studied this matter closely in the Bible.

Later when I saw the manifestations of the Spirit in others, I realized that what I experienced in 1902 of the power of God accompanied by speaking in tongues was the baptism in the Holy Spirit. It is not any more remarkable than that.

Many people are hindered from receiving the baptism in the Holy Spirit because they are expecting something which, as far as they are concerned, never will come. They are expecting violent outward manifestations, but they are waiting in vain. In my case the power came upon me very unexpectedly when I, for the first time, experienced this power and spoke in tongues. When I was in Oslo in February of 1907, I prayed for the baptism in the Holy Spirit. I expected then to have a very remarkable experience with great outward manifestations, but they never came. In one way I left Kristiania disappointed, because I had not experienced the physical manifestation of the baptism in the Holy Spirit which I had expected. Nevertheless, in my personal relationship to God and to my environment, wonderful things had transpired which would be of great future importance to my life.

I passed through a period of heart-searching in my own life. What concerned me more than anything was whether there was anything in my life which hindered the divine power I desired to experience. As I have stated before, I had from my earliest years a longing to be used in the Lord's work. It was for that purpose I desired the power of God. One incident from that time has always been quite vivid in my mind.

One night while I was in Kristiania, Pastor Barratt preached in the Tabernacle, the Baptist church. I had been a member of this church for many years so that just about everyone there knew me. I felt this was the right time and place to request prayer for myself, so I made known my condition. I felt my nothingness as a Christian, and I realized that there was much more spiritual equipment available for a witness for Christ.

At the end of the service we knelt in prayer, and Pastor Barratt came to me. He had heard my request for prayer that God would make me better fitted as a preacher of the Gospel. This was apparently the reason he directed three questions to me: "Are you willing to be anything for Jesus? Are you willing to do anything for Jesus? Are you willing to go anywhere for Jesus?"

I did not reply immediately but pondered the meaning of these questions. I thought: "This is just like committing suicide. I'll throw away my entire life." Then the thought struck me, "But what's going to become of your life, if you don't receive the divine power you're longing for?" It is remarkable how fast a person can think on such an occasion. It seemed as though I reviewed my entire life during the few seconds I was silent and kept Pastor Barratt waiting for my answer.

My choice was made, and broken before God, I answered: "Yea, I will be anything! Yes, I will do anything!

"I will go anywhere for Jesus, if He gives me the power I need."

In response, Pastor Barratt laid his hands on me and

prayed for me, but I did not feel anything special, although I knew that something had happened. I had taken another step along God's way.

There was another matter which troubled me much in those days. I had a girl friend with whom I had corresponded for five years. Now I had a feeling that if God were to have His way in my life, I had to be absolutely independent so I could decide about myself and my actions. I was very fond of her, and she had everything I wanted my future wife to have, but in this situation I felt it was necessary to be free so that I would not be bound by any interests other than my life's calling as a servant of God.

I had written to her before I went to Kristiania and asked her to meet me there, which she also had done. We attended the services together during the days and at night. She was possessed with the same interest and longing for spiritual things as I. Now, however, I felt strongly that it would be a handicap to be attached to another person by my side, a person I would have to consider in my desire to do the will of God in everything.

I placed this matter before her. To begin with she thought that this revival had driven me to the extreme position of being determined to remain single. She argued with me and pointed out that Pastor Barratt was married, and he was a man whom God used. My intention, however, was not celibacy as such; I was only concerned about full freedom to go God's way without any consideration to close relatives. She understood, and in prayer before God we broke the secret engagement, as the Norwegians termed our relationship. From that day we left each other. I bought her a Bible as a remembrance and told her: "If I ever marry I will first of all inquire about you." This was a sincere promise!

She was a remarkably wonderful girl. When I think of the loose relationships between young people which are advocated by many today, I can only say that such looseness was unthinkable as far as we were concerned. Still what wonderful times we had together! Now, however, she accepted my action as God's way for us and was satisfied with what had been done. She returned to her home in Kragero, Norway, and a year later she went to America. Neither she nor any of her family ever questioned my strange action, and this is something I always appreciated very much.

Five years went by, during which time the foundation was laid for my future and the work to which I dedicated my life with everything I was and had. I spent four and a half years of that time in Lidkoping, Vastergotland, in Sweden.

The church in that city was a comparatively small one, and I had much opportunity for studies. Apart from sermon preparation and some visitation I spent all my time in reading the Holy Scriptures. I had no family and could devote many hours to increasing my knowledge in the Word and in church history. It was a wonderful time.

Then I moved to Stockholm and took my stand regarding doctrinal and denominational questions. As the work in the capital grew I realized that this would be my future field of service. Then I decided that the time had come to consider marriage. In the month of May in 1912, I wrote a letter to my future mother-in-law and asked for the address of the girl I had broken up with in Kristiania in 1907. We had not corresponded for five years; she had only sent a card to me when my mother passed away in 1908, but she had not given any return address, so I was unable to answer.

Now her mother sent me the address, and I wrote to her in America. I didn't know if she was engaged or married, and she had not given me any promise when we parted ways. Consequently my first letter was for purposes of investigation. In my second letter I asked if she would be willing to come home and be united with me. In April, 1913, we were married. All our friends know about the unique pattern of life we experienced during fifty-four happy years. God blessed our union with ten children, nine of whom are still alive. They also speak of their childhood on the little farm outside of Stockholm as a bright fairy tale. On December 30, 1966, my life's companion went to be with the

Lord after she had completed a wonderful life.

My attitude toward my marriage was of great importance in the success of my work. It was absolutely clear to me that unfaithfulness toward her and the promise I had given her would rob me of the blessing I enjoyed in my life and ministry. During the first years of the Pentecostal revival I was often invited to conventions. At such time invitations were given to me, and even parents were speaking on behalf of their daughters, but on my part there was never a thought of breaking my promise to Lydia Danielsen who later became my wife. We married by faith in God, a faith we later had opportunity to practice.

When I asked her how she could be so relaxed during the five years we never corresponded and why she did not become attached to someone else, she responded that she thought God was in this, and she was interested in seeing how it all would end. She was a wonderful woman of faith!

All of this ties in with the Pentecostal revival in Kristiania and my surrender to God, and it was of tremendous importance to my ministry; and it actually happened as a consequence of the baptism in the Holy Spirit.

## IMPORTANT FORKS IN THE ROAD

No spiritual experience delivers us from temptations, neither can an experience be so altogether convincing that it removes all possibility of our doubting its genuineness. We can find many proofs of this statement in the Bible.

John the Baptist had had the most wonderful experience of Jesus and His Messianic call. He had also given a clear testimony of Him as the Lamb of God which takes away the sin of the world. He had preached that Jesus was the Son of God, and that He was the coming Bridegroom. Still, at a later date, he questioned all of this. Sitting in a prison alone John thought that the whole situation seemed like a riddle. Therefore he requested one of his own disciples, who visited him in prison, to ask Jesus: "Art thou he that should come, or do we look for another?" (Matt. 11:3).

Those must have been dark days for the bold proclaimer of Christ; now he was sitting alone and forsaken in the cellar of a huge desert fort which also served as the palace of Herod. How could Christ reveal such a marvelous authority in His speaking and in His miracles and at the same time allow His fellow soldier to languish at the caprice of these morally depraved and cruel people? Doubt has a passkey that fits every lock. No faith, no experience and no fear of God can shut it out.

Before the Pentecostal movement in 1907, I had a sincere longing to live for God, and I had experienced so many encouraging and faith-building things, that one might have expected that I would be absolutely sure of myself. But doubt came to me also with a tremendous force; it happened while I attended the Bethel Seminary, the ministerial school of the Swedish Baptist denomination. When I had covered my assignments I spent a great deal of time in the library of the school. There I had opportunity to read literature with which I was not formerly acquainted. Amongst other works, I read one by Victor Rydberg, a Swedish thinker, who tried to demonstrate that Christ Himself never claimed to be divine. It shook me. If I had read that book now, it would in no way affect my faith. At that time, however, I did not have the Bible knowledge I now possess. Therefore the arguments shook my faith in Christ and in the Bible.

My association with the other students was no good influence on my spiritual life either. No longer did I live that victorious and happy life I had done before. This changed my entire outlook and placed me in a different spiritual position. I questioned my call to the ministry, and for some time I was considering a change to devote my life to altogether different interests.

It seemed to me to be sheer falsehood to preach the Gospel if it cannot be supported by the divine and eternal realities of which the Bible speaks. During these doubts I lost all joy and power in my Christian life, and I could easily see that such a shaky position would never endure, as far as I was concerned. My soul became the battleground of inner conflicts. I had to find a clear answer. Is the Bible the Word of God and is Christ the One He said He was?

I had never had any doubts regarding God as the Creator. The thesis that this wonderful universe had created itself I never could accept. But I had received so many doubts in my heart about the Bible and Christ that I simply had to find a clear answer to these questions.

I said to myself, "If I cannot find absolute assurance that the Bible's portrayal of Christ is reliable I will throw away this book and never have anything to do with such fraud as preaching the Gospel. But if I can be convinced that Christ is the One He said He is, and that the Bible's view of God is true, then I will give my life one hundred percent to God and His cause."

This crisis eventually came to an end and I found release through prayer, as in my previous spiritual experiences. All alone in a little attic room I was prostrate on the floor fighting an inner battle, looking for a clear answer. Right then and there I had a personal meeting with Jesus. I did not see him with my physical eye, but I experienced His presence. When that encounter had taken place I knew that I had met Him. And remarkably enough, all my doubts disappeared, and they have never more troubled me. This was also the occasion for a powerful spiritual renewing, bringing power to live for God and to serve Him. All this happened shortly before the Pentecostal beginnings in 1907.

From then on, my spiritual experience became much richer. At that time I came across a couple of books which were of great help to me – Charles G. Finney's *Autobiography* and a volume by A. J. Gordon on *The Twofold Life.* These two books spoke of a richer spiritual life than was generally lived and preached in the circles where I moved. Strangely enough I did not come to a clear understanding of the Pentecostal teaching in spite of this type of reading. Neither did it lead me to a comprehension of what happened to me personally when the Spirit fell on me in 1902. The reason for this was probably that I felt the authors of these volumes which I had read must have had much greater experiences than I had received.

From that time a far greater power than before accompanied my ministry. The results I saw in my ministry were to a large extent of the same character as those which have been typical of my ministry all through the years. There was one outstanding difference, however, between my ministry before and after 1907. I cannot recall that anyone was baptized in the Holy Spirit in my services during 1905-1906.

Certainty of faith and a glowing zeal for the salvation of men characterized my preaching and my services. I had a special burden for young people who were beset by doubt, and I had the privilege of leading many of them to a living faith in God.

The joy which this assurance of faith gives was a noticeable strength in my life and ministry from that time on.

* * *

Once again, however, I was to be tempted to leave the ministry. The life of a preacher never was particularly attractive to me. If I had felt free to choose another way I would have done so probably at any given time during my life.

One of the things which gave me a great deal of respect for marriage and the responsibility for a family was the financial side. I envisioned myself as a pastor of a small and poor church, where of necessity I would have to live in want and poverty. Therefore, I did not marry until I was pastoring a church of five hundred members and felt I would have an income adequate to support a family.

Let me repeat again, however, that as far as I am concerned, there has never been any special attraction in the position of a pastor. If I had not had such a strong consciousness of a divine call, I would never have continued in this work to which I have dedicated my entire life. In spite of this attitude of mine, I must say that I have loved my calling. Spiritual factors, however, shaped my life in this direction.

I was very much at home with my work and ministry in Vastergotland, my home province of Sweden. We had a wonderful time there. The little assembly I served grew from fifty to one hundred and fifty members, and I had a feeling I could have continued in that church for the rest of my life. When I had been there for four years, however, I came into a serious crisis. Again I reviewed the question as to whether I should continue as a preacher. These thoughts troubled me for a long time. I had several preliminary inquiries from different directions, such as from Pastor John Ongman in Orebro who wanted me to be his co-worker and from the nucleus in Stockholm which later was to develop into the Filadelfia Church. But I had given a negative reply to these inquiries. I was very much inclined to quit the ministry. For a long time I prayed about this matter and I promised God that I would preach in my spare time, work with the ministry of music, etc. I did not feel, however, that I wanted the responsibility of a church and its many activities.

It is possible that I was exhausted and tired and that this endeavor to get away from the ministry was a reaction that caused this weariness. But I felt that my endeavor to leave the ministry was meant seriously. I had even secured a secular position which was waiting for me.

At that time I had a dream — a vision which made an indelible impression on me. I lived in a little prophet's chamber and slept on a wooden sofa which was placed alongside the wall to the right of the door. In my vision I saw two of my best friends, Rev. O.L. Bjork and Rev. Oskar Janson, enter the door and stop at the foot of the sofa. Both of them looked at me, with deep seriousness reflected in their faces, and Rev. Bjork said: "If therefore the light that is in thee be darkness, how great is that darkness!"

When they turned around and left the room I was awake,

and I felt deeply shaken by this surprising experience. I lit the kerosene lantern on the table and saw that it was 6 o'clock in the morning. I could not recall where the Scripture was found which Rev. Bjork had quoted, so I turned to my concordance and found it in the Sermon on the Mount (Matt. 6:23). Immediately, I comprehended the relationship between this strange experience and my efforts to leave the ministry.

After I realized what time it was and had read the Scripture which had been cited, I threw myself on my knees and asked God to forgive me for my endeavors to run away from my call. There I surrendered myself anew to God and to the ministry He might have for me.

The same day this happened, I went to a conference in Orebro. Upon my return I found a letter on my table with a call from the Filadelfia Church in Stockholm. The church had been formed about a week before the call was extended to me. The membership was around 30.

When Albert Engsell, who actually had taken the initiative in founding the Filadelfia Church, first asked me to come and be their pastor, I had given an emphatic "no" as my answer. I was so attached to the work in Vastergotland that I had no thought of moving. But it was then that this depression gripped me, and I was so totally detached from the work there that I had made preparations for a secular position.

The call from Stockholm had been prepared through the little assembly's prayers and fasting, and it found me prepared because of my recent experiences. The battle I fought and the temptation to leave the ministry and shepherding of a flock was, so I later realized, a preparation for the call which was to lead to my life's calling and work.

## SPEAKING IN TONGUES

The gift of the Spirit which has attracted most of the attention surrounding the Pentecostal revival is speaking in tongues. It has become the object of much opposition and has been the cause of a continual debate. This is quite natural for several different reasons.

This gift is the most mysterious of the nine gifts the apostle Paul speaks about. Already on the first day of Pentecost it produced a great sensation and was responsible for the fact that Peter's sermon to a large extent became an apologetic answer. The matter involved basic issues, and therefore he dealt with them and answered them with references to the Scriptures as well as with logic.

Tongues speaking is on a different level than many of the other gifts. It is a gift dedicated to our prayer life. Its sphere is the spirit of man, or what the psychologists call the subconscious. It is more spontaneous than any other gift and operates with ease in the right atmosphere.

When a person who has the gift of speaking in tongues enters a setting where the Holy Spirit is at work, he is gripped by the atmosphere surrounding him, and he may begin quite naturally to speak in tongues. His spirit is moved upon and he joins in the prevailing spirit of prayer and praise.

In the 14th chapter of First Corinthians the apostle Paul has given us the most detailed instructions in this area:

"For he that speaketh in an unknown tongue speaketh not unto men, but unto God: for no man understandeth him; howbeit in the spirit he speaketh mysteries.

"But he that prophesieth speaketh unto men to edification, and exhortation, and comfort.

"He that speaketh in an unknown tongue edifieth himself; but he that prophesieth edifieth the church. . . .

"Wherefore let him that speaketh in an unknown tongue pray that he may interpret.

"For if I pray in an unknown tongue, my spirit prayeth but my understanding is unfruitful.

"What is it then? I will pray with the spirit, and I will pray with the understanding also: I will sing with the spirit, and I will sing with the understanding also.

"Else when thou shalt bless with the spirit, how shall he that occupieth the room of the unlearned say Amen at thy giving of thanks, seeing he understandeth not what thou sayest?

"For thou verily givest thanks well, but the other is not edified" (I Cor. 14:2-4; 13-17).

I have included this long quotation from Paul's famous writing which shows that tongues speaking belongs to the prayer life, the communication men can enjoy with the divine world. Paul says that it is speaking "not unto men, but unto God." This speaking to God he characterizes as prayer, praise, and singing in the Spirit – consequently a communication with God.

He also recommends that the one who speaks in tongues should pray that he may interpret in order that the church might understand the prayer and the praise and be able to say Amen to the thanksgiving. Consequently, we see that Paul held that when tongues speaking is interpreted it will be prayer, praise, and thanksgiving. The interpretation should not change the contents of the tongues utterance but simply render it in an intelligible language.

Those who have read what our psychologists have published in the last few years concerning their findings in this area realize how much of this realm still is unexplored. What is called science in this field to a great extent is nothing but guesses. The findings they have presented are based on frail functions. The personal testimonies and the research which have been rendered have proven so shallow and questionable that one is surprised that such work can pass as science. I am referring to the psychological research published by some Swedish scientists concerning speaking in tongues in the Pentecostal movement.

While speaking in tongues is mysterious it is no more difficult to understand than some other phenomena related to the psychological realm, such as the very common phenomenon of prayer. This is a spiritual manifestation of life which is found among all people. The human spirit – the non-materialisic within man – in that way expresses its desire for higher values, and this desire can be turned in different directions. The believer in God turns it toward divinity and finds satisfaction.

The subconscious in man is generally governed by a spirit which more or less asserts itself in the everyday life. When man's thought no longer controls his words then the subconscious appears. The swearing man while fully awake may reflect his inner world in oaths which are not the result of his thought, but rather a spontaneous flow over his lips. If one would reprove him for doing it, he might excuse himself and say in his defense that he was not thinking of what he said. Cursing to him is a spontaneous expression of what he has on the inside. In an unguarded moment this then becomes an expression of what he thinks and feels in his innermost being.

As the swearing man is ruled by the powers he calls on in his curses, so the Spirit-baptized man is ruled by the Spirit of God, to whom he spontaneously renders his prayer and praise. Some have criticized the Spirit-filled for the praises that often are upon their lips.

At the beginning of the revival we were criticized for praising God so much, and I began to look into the praise I personally rendered without thinking of what I was doing. Were they possibly right who claimed that our praise was nothing but a habit, a routine jargon of no value? But then and there I met a number of Scriptures about prayer in the Spirit. Jesus taught His disciples that "men ought always to pray, and not to faint" (Luke 18:1). The apostle Paul said: "Praying always with all prayer and supplication in the Spirit" (Eph. 6:18), and "Pray without ceasing" (I Thess. 5:17).

When the life in the fullness of the Spirit has become the natural way of life for a person, it is also a normal condition for him to praise God when he is alone, and when he is with people. This is his atmosphere, his breath of life — to have fellowship with God and spontaneously express it.

One need never be afraid that this spontaneous praise is hypocritical. The hypocrite thinks of what he is doing, but the spontaneous and unpremeditated is a sound expression of what dwells in the inner world of man.

He who walks in the Spirit, as the Scripture says, to him it is natural to live this continual prayer life with spontaneous praise and thanksgiving. This is, of course, the only way in which one can always be praying in the Spirit.

It is in this area that speaking in tongues has its foremost place. The Bible states: "He that speaketh in an unknown tongue edifieth himself" (I Cor. 14:4). This is the first great purpose of this gift. It is given as an instrument for prayer in the Spirit. It also will serve in the united prayer when the church is gathered in either closed or public meetings. This will be true on the condition that he who prays or praises God in tongues can interpret his utterance so that the church can share its contents. It may also be so that someone other than the person who speaks in tongues has the gift of interpretation and can interpret the tongues utterance.

There has often been speaking with tongues followed by what one thought was an interpretation, but which was in reality a prophecy, because the Scripture plainly teaches, "He that speaketh in an unknown tongue speaketh not unto men, but unto God" (I Cor. 14:2). Then some feel that such a manifestation of the Spirit is false, but it need not be anything other than just a misunderstanding of what one is experiencing. What one assumes to be the interpretation of the tongues utterance is a prophecy altogether independent of the speaking in tongues. The loss in such a case is that one does not get the interpretation of the tongues which, no doubt, was a prayer or praise of great value. The church in that case loses the edification which it probably was in great need of.

It may also happen that an interpretation fails to be brought forth simply because the interpreter thinks that a prayer or praise cannot be the correct interpretation. He is expecting a message to the people. When this does not come to him he finds it hard to accept the inspiration to prayer and praise which he feels to be the true interpretation of the utterance in tongues.

Doubts regarding the reality of spiritual gifts have often arisen because people have confused prophecy and interpretation of tongues. There may come an utterance of tongues followed by an exhortation to the congregation, and it, somehow, does not seem to agree with the tongues. The message which followed was neither of the same length nor of the same spirit as the speaking in tongues. Such incidents may cause doubts. Remember, however, that the first was a tongues utterance which was a prayer or praise while the other was an independent prophetic message.

A correct understanding of the much-discussed speaking in tongues is of tremendous importance both to the life of the individual and that of the church. Even as the prayer life is very important in this respect so is also the gift which is given particularly for the purpose of deepening and strengthening the prayer life. What a blessing for the individual to speak to God in this manner. "He that speaketh in an unknown tongue," the apostle Paul says, "edifieth himself" – and himself alone – unless the tongues utterance is interpreted. When interpretation follows, the whole church can be edified.

This gift is a sign "to them that believe not" (I Cor. 14:22). It is a sign which in a remarkable way can attract the attention of those that doubt, and it has served as an alarm clock since the first appearance of Christianity.

* * *

Ever since the Pentecostal revival of this 20th century began in America there has been a discussion regarding speaking in tongues as the evidence of the baptism in the Holy Spirit. In some circles it has been established as the accepted doctrine, and it has been preached as one of the tenets of the Pentecostal revival. The result has been that many have fixed their attention altogether too much on speaking in tongues and have drifted away from that which really leads the experience, the baptism in the Holy Spirit.

The New Testament Scriptures which treat this aspect of the truth do not explicitly make any such statement. It appears, however, that again and again where the Holy Spirit fell, people spoke in tongues. We have also observed in our experience that where the Spirit falls, people speak in tongues, although we have never made this a point of doctrine.

It is also written that "these signs shall follow them that believe" (Mark 16:17). Faith and experience precede and the signs follow. We must receive the baptism in the Holy Spirit by faith in the same manner and on the same conditions as we receive the forgiveness of sins. We never tell an unconverted person when we lead him to Christ that he is to seek a sign or an evidence of his salvation. We teach him to believe the promises and praise God for the forgiveness of sins, even though he may not feel anything. In like manner we receive the baptism in the Holy Spirit by faith, and we claim that we have that which we ask for. When faith becomes real and living to our hearts we will experience the baptism in the Holy Spirit. If we follow this way of the Bible, simple but straight, Jesus will baptize us in the Holy Spirit. We can be sure that He will give us everything that belongs to the baptism in the Holy Spirit.

A journalist on one occasion asked Pastor T.B. Barratt of Oslo, Norway, "Do you still believe in the baptism in the Holy Spirit?"

"Yes," replied Pastor Barratt.

"Do you believe that speaking in tongues is the evidence of the baptism in the Holy Spirit?"

"Yes," answered the pastor again, "I still do."

"But," objected the journalist, "don't you believe, Pastor Barratt, that there could be some exceptions to that rule?"

"Yes," Pastor Barratt admitted, "there is no rule without exceptions," but he added, "I don't want to be that exception."

# The Outpouring Of The Spirit Upon All Flesh

### Joel's Prophecy

### IT SHALL COME TO PASS AFTERWARD ...

#### I

It is obvious that with Israel's return to their ancient land, the land which God once promised Abraham, new light has been shed on the biblical prophecies concerning the end-time events. While the evolving world situation in a remarkable way has served the interests of Antichrist, and while ever stronger forces have been employed to dismiss Christ from the scene of our world, the end result, at the same time, points in the opposite direction.

Cruel persecutions and efforts to exterminate the Jewish people scattered among the nations of the world have threatened their very existence, but in the midst of such adversities this little people has reached its millennial aspiration to return to the land of their fathers. And more than that — through a remarkable chain of events, which no one can satisfactorily explain — Israel is today the focal point of all current, international politics.

Every thinking person, who will give even a little attention to the Bible's predictions concerning this subject, realizes that there is an invisible hand behind the course of world events.

My intention is not to cover all of the complex questions related to Israel's role in the last days, to the coming of Christ and to the final triumph of His kingdom. God does, however, have a plan for His entire world! As we discover order in all of nature in the minutest details as well as in the larger contexts, so we find both basic and detailed blueprints for all of God's works. In His systematic plan He includes, not only the individual, the church and Israel, but also all the peoples and nations of the world.

Once long ago, God gave the great Nebuchadnezzar a reminder of this divine world map, which indicated not only the name of the kingdoms but also their place in history. God informed this ruler of the order in which these world-empires would succeed each other and of Christ's kingdom as the final act in the great drama of the world.

"Daniel answered in the presence of the king, and said, The secret which the king hath demanded cannot the wise men, the astrologers, the magicians, the soothsayers, shew unto the king;

"But there is a God in heaven that revealeth secrets, and maketh known to the king Nebuchadnezzar what shall be in the latter days. Thy dream, and the visions of thy head upon thy bed, are these;

"As for thee, O king, thy thoughts came into thy mind upon thy bed, what should come to pass hereafter: and he that revealeth secrets maketh known to thee what shall come to pass.

"But as for me, this secret is not revealed to me for any wisdom that I have more than any living, but for their sakes that shall make known the interpretation to the king, and that thou mightest know the thoughts of thy heart.

"Thou, O king, sawest, and behold a great image. This great image, whose brightness was excellent, stood before thee; and the form thereof was terrible.

"This image's head was of fine gold, his breast and his arms of silver, his belly and his thighs of brass,

"His legs of iron, his feet part of iron and part of clay.

"Thou sawest till that a stone was cut out without hands, which smote the image upon his feet that were of iron and clay, and brake them to pieces.

"Then was the iron, the clay, the brass, the silver, and the gold, broken to pieces together, and became like the chaff of the summer threshing floors; and the wind carried them away, that no place was found for them: and the stone that smote the image became a great mountain, and filled the whole earth.

"This is the dream; and we will tell the interpretation thereof before the king.

"Thou, O king, art a king of kings: for the God of heaven hath given thee a kingdom, power, and strength, and glory.

"And wheresoever the children of men dwell, the beasts of the field and the fowls of the heaven hath he given into thine hand, and hath made thee ruler over them all. Thou art this head of gold.

"And after thee shall arise another kingdom inferior to thee, and another third kingdom of brass, which shall rule over all the earth.

"And the fourth kingdom shall be strong as iron: forasmuch as iron breaketh in pieces and subdueth all things: and as iron that breaketh all these, shall it break in pieces and bruise.

"And whereas thou sawest the feet and toes, part of potters' clay, and part of iron, the kingdom shall be divided; but there shall be in it of the strength of the iron, forasmuch as thou sawest the iron mixed with miry clay.

"And as the toes of the feet were part of iron, and part of clay, so the kingdom shall be partly strong, and partly broken.

"And whereas thou sawest iron mixed with miry clay, they shall mingle themselves with the seed of men: but they shall not cleave one to another, even as iron is not mixed with clay.

"And in the days of these kings shall the God of heaven set up a kingdom, which shall never be destroyed: and the kingdom shall not be left to other people, but it shall break in pieces and consume all these kingdoms, and it shall stand for ever.

"Forasmuch as thou sawest that the stone was cut out of

the mountain without hands, and that it brake in pieces the iron, the brass, the clay, the silver, and the gold; the great God hath made known to the king what shall come to pass hereafter: and the dream is certain, and the interpretation thereof sure" (Dan. 2:27-45).

This entire plan issues in the victory of God's and Christ's kingdom. In this kingdom both Israel and the church play a part. It is all included in the kingdom Christ proclaimed when he first appeared and said: "Repent, for the kingdom of heaven is at hand."

Between this kingdom and the materialistic and Antichrist forces, a struggle has been going on ever since the fall, and it will continue until Christ has won the final victory.

This plan is actually also a war plan which was seen by the prophets in their visions and then shared with their contemporaries and recorded for their posterity. A plan of war is generally developed in such a way that it will be difficult to understand, just in case it should fall into the hands of the enemy. Those who have the key to the strategic language of prophecy, who have the secret code, they – and they alone–understand this plan of war.

In keeping with this, we conclude that the key to the prophecy of Joel is a thoroughgoing knowledge of Israel's history. With this key in our hand, we can see the entire goal and purpose in the divine plan for the world.

In the last days the nations of the world will have their part in the great drama just exactly like Babylon, Medo-Persia, Greece, and Rome according to Daniel's prophecy. Among these, the fifth world power, the kingdom of God, will take its place and fight the battles of the Lord. Israel and Christianity will combine their forces with the armies of the supernatural world.

When that time comes the Holy Spirit will be a decisive factor, and God will pour out of His Spirit upon all flesh. It is therefore my intention especially to keep in focus the spiritual revival which will run like a red thread throughout all the remarkable events of the last days.

A couple of years ago, when once again reading through the prophecy of Joel, I discovered something which I had never noticed before. Over the years I had in Joel's book particularly given my attention to the prophecy concerning the outpouring of the Spirit, which Peter cited on the day of Pentecost. As a leader in a Christian movement where the experience of the baptism in the Holy Spirit has been strongly emphasized, I have, of course, often referred to this prophecy and stressed the viewpoints that are usual in Pentecostal ranks.

At this particular reading, however, my attention was fixed on one word which I had never really noticed in this prophetic message, namely the word "afterward" (Joel 2:28). I realized that this word reveals a definite determination of time. Certain events in Israel's history would take place before others would follow. Among the latter the prophet mentions that God will pour out of His Spirit upon all flesh. This is the first significant event he predicts that will follow Israel's return to her own land.

As always when discovering something new in the Word of God, I experienced joy in a great measure; but it was more than that. This word gave me an outlook on this prophetic area of truth which inspired me to a new search in the Scriptures concerning this subject.

Upon giving myself to a more careful study of Joel than ever before, I discovered that the prophet in the early parts of his prophecy covers Israel's history in a very concentrated form until the day this people will have returned to their country. He points out certain great historic events, describes God's ways with His people, and tells how through the ages Israel has reacted to God's dealings with them.

The prophets who described the future course of events did not confine their salvation message only to Israel but included the whole world. The prophets in old Israel broke the theological isolation which the legalistic scribes proclaimed, and they included all the world in God's love and care. Joel is such a prophet who has a powerful message not only about Israel's return to their own land but also about a glorious outpouring of the Holy Spirit upon the entire world. He also brings both of these events together in a very interesting context.

What has happened and is happening in Israel tells us that God keeps His promises, and that the people of the promise will play a role in the historical course of events. This reminds us of that great biblical thought, that God is the God not only of the church, but of Israel and of all the world. Behind the march of history which sometimes appears so capricious is, as earlier stated, an unseen hand which will not let go of its hold. God says, "At the time I have appointed I will render fair judgments, The earth is quaking with all its inhabitants; I have set firm its pillars" (Ps. 75:2, 3 Berk. ver.).

The current events in and around Israel are signs of the times. Although the sand in God's hourglass seems to run slowly, nevertheless, it shows correct time. The present-day events in the near East tell us the time of God's clock. Israel's return to their land and the annexation of the whole city of Jerusalem mark the beginning of a new historical epoch.

Many Christians have held that when Christ's words in Luke 21:24 would be fulfilled, the time of the second coming of the Lord would be here. Jesus says concerning this: "And they shall fall by the edge of the sword, and shall be led away captive into all nations: and Jerusalem shall be trodden down of the Gentiles, until the times of the Gentiles be fulfilled." Such an interpretation of this passage must be erroneous, for Jesus adds: "And when these things begin to come to pass, then look up, and lift up your heads; for your redemption draweth nigh" (Luke 21:28).

The expression "the times of the Gentiles" has been interpreted in various ways. Some maintain that "the times of the Gentiles" began when Nebuchadnezzar occupied Jerusalem and brought Israel as captives to Babylon around 587-586 B.C. Others believe that "the times of the Gentiles" comprise the time from Israel's bondage in Egypt until the second coming of Christ. It has also been referred to as the time when the message of God and of His plan of salvation would be proclaimed, not by Israel, but by the Christian Gentile church.

Whatever interpretation we may have, the land is now in the possession of the Israelis, and Jerusalem is no longer "trodden down of the Gentiles" but belongs entirely to Israel. "The times of the Gentiles" have been fulfilled. God is again counting with Israel. A new era has begun.

One thing certainly cannot be misinterpreted, namely, that God stands firmly behind His Word and keeps what He has promised. Therefore the whole world can rest assured that the promise of an outpouring of the Spirit upon all flesh is of the same character and same firmness as the promise He gave to Abraham and which He through His prophets renewed all through the ages.

The two promises which God gave through the prophet Joel — the promise that Israel would return to their land and the promise of an outpouring of the Holy Spirit upon all flesh — belong together as two inseparable events, as two halves of the same promise. One shall first be fulfilled and "afterward" the other follows without any reservation.

This revelation in Joel has come to me as a surprising discovery, as a solution to difficult riddles, and as a floodlight throwing its beam upon a future veiled in changing and obscure opinions.

## II

Joel's prophecy is a seer's hurried sketch of what he beholds in the future. From the mount of revelation he peers through 2,700 years to our days and describes events which we of this generation can see before our very eyes. His description of people is so varied, original and dramatic that it is unique in all of mankind's history. Concentrated as in a nutshell we find the most important and most decisive events in Israel's extraordinary wanderings through three thousand years.

When the prophet has permitted us to see Israel's history pass before us as in a review until we find Israel in their ancient land, possessing the whole city of Jerusalem, he exclaims: "And it shall come to pass *afterward . . .*"

Thus the prophet's interesting description presents a panorama of the most important events in Israel's history until our days.

Under David and Solomon the nation of Israel enjoyed great success. The little country was strong, respected and successful in every way. The secret was that their kings believed in God and counted with Him, in spite of their own great weaknesses. Their faith in God and their loyal worship of the true and living God was the secret of Israel's prosperity and good fortune at that time.

Later, however, there came a time when the kings led the people astray. They ended in idolatry and in a spiritual and moral declension. There were also times of visitation, as in the days of Elijah who ministered in Judah and of Elisha who preached among the ten tribes in Samaria; those were days when the people had been led away from their faith in God to worship Baal. Jesus refers to this period as an example of how a nation can shut itself out from spiritual and temporal blessings, in spite of the fact that the people know the will of God and are gifted with chosen instruments from God who proclaim the divine truth and warn of judgment to come (Luke 4:25-27). In such a manner Israel squandered both spiritual and material blessings through their pride and their faithlessness toward God.

Their punishment came in the form of physical difficulties. Famine ravaged. It came either by lack of precipitation or by insects or animals which devoured the crops. The great famine of those days was an outstanding event in Israel's history, and that is the reason why it is given such a prominent place on the prophetic map (Joel 1:4-5).

The next great event in Israel's history which we find in Joel's vision is the Babylonian exile when the king of Judah, his family, and his people were led captive to that foreign land. The kingdom of Israel in Samaria had already fallen to the Assyrians (II Chron. 17:6-14). Joel refers to this tragedy: "For a nation is come up upon my land, strong, and without number, whose teeth are the teeth of a lion, and he hath the cheek teeth of a great lion" (Joel 1:6).

The Babylonian empire reached its highest point of power and splendor under Nebuchadnezzar. The walls and the hanging gardens have been lauded by Horace. An eloquent orator said that, walking down Babylon's main street, one must have had the impression that the very clouds were in bloom, and the very heavens leaned on the shoulders of the mighty cedars.

Babylon's symbol was a lion, and above the gate into the city's main street was the image of a lion on enameled tiles, which now belong to the collections of archeologists. It was the might of the young Nebuchadnezzar and of his empire Joel described.

The Babylonian captivity made a deep incision in Israel's history, and its consequences have in many ways marked the continued development of the Jewish people.

One of the results was the impoverishment of the country after the people had been exiled. During seventy years the land deteriorated as described by Joel in verses 7-12 of the first chapter. The lamentations of Israel by the rivers in Babylon have been interpreted by the poets in the Book of Psalms.

When the hour of liberation came, the spiritually alert accepted and took advantage of the opportunity to return. Nehemiah's and Ezra's initiative, and the permission by Cyrus to rebuild the city and the temple, however, were ignored by the great masses of Israel. While millions of Jews, the affluent and wealthy, remained in the country around the Euphrates with its prospering economy, according to contemporary historians, only about 50,000 returned to their impoverished homeland. Joel alludes to this in his description:

"Gird yourselves, and lament, ye priests: howl, ye

ministers of the altar: come, lie all night in sackcloth, ye ministers of my God: for the meat offering and the drink offering is withholden from the house of your God. Sanctify ye a fast, call a solemn assembly, gather the elders and all the inhabitants of the land into the house of the Lord your God, and cry unto the Lord" (Joel 1:13, 14). (I confess I don't quite see it.)

For those who considered it a mighty miracle of God, it was a keen disappointment to see how the great majority of Israel reacted to the mercy of deliverance which God had extended to them.

Later as a people in their own land they experienced defeats and humiliations which the prophet could not neglect to mention in his visions into the future. Such a milestone of misfortune was the reign of terror under Antiochus IV Epiphanes.

"Alas for the day! for the day of the Lord is at hand, and as a destruction from the Almighty shall it come" (Joel 1:15).

This Syrian despot wanted to heathenize Israel and force upon them heathen customs and practices. He prohibited circumcision and commanded that swine should be sacrificed in the temple at Jerusalem.

This was the cause of the guerrilla fighting, spearheaded by the Maccabees, which once again led to the independence of the state of Israel. Internal feuds between the Jews weakened the nation until Rome occupied the country. During all these crises there were times of spiritual, political and material distress.

The spiritual need was especially depressing, and the prophet seeing this asks: "Is not the meat cut off before our eyes, yea, joy and gladness from the house of our God?" (Joel 1:16). The people had lost their blessing of being God's people, and the center of their worship, the temple in Jerusalem, had sunk in the deepest humiliation.

When the Romans occupied Jerusalem, the temple was violated in a humiliating way. Pompey defiled it by entering into the most holy place, where none but the priest could enter once a year.

Also under Herod the Great there was a time of declension in spite of the fact that he rebuilt the temple. This he did to satisfy personal ambitions and to gain political advantages among the people. But at the same time he built a theater in the city and a circus outside the city walls. His evil-doings and cruelties are well-known both from secular history and from the New Testament. After his death, around the time Christ was born, the political power was inherited by his sons, although the country still remained under Roman authority. This was a time of spiritual drought and political insecurity and oppression. Tributary kings and tetrarchs poisoned the very existence of the people by their personal ambitions and cruelty. "Joy and gladness" had departed "from the house of our God" (Joel 1:16). Such was the general condition when Jesus made His public appearance.

When Christ came, He preached a "year of the Lord's favor" (Luke 4:19 Berk. ver.). But through the resistance of the spiritual leaders of that time Jesus was compelled to pronounce severe judgments upon His own people.

At the close of His earthly sojourn Jesus sat upon the Mount of Olives, and looking out over the city of Jerusalem, He wept and said: "If thou hadst known, even thou, at least in this thy day, the things which belong unto thy peace! but now they are hid from thine eyes. For the days shall come upon thee, that thine enemies shall cast a trench about thee, and compass thee round, and keep thee in on every side, And shall lay thee even with the ground, and thy children within thee; and they shall not leave in thee one stone upon another; because thou knewest not the time of thy visitation" (Luke 19:42-44).

This was a day of the Lord when God in a special way visited His people, but they rejected Him and it became the severest day of judgment Israel up to that time had experienced. They denied and rejected the Son of God, the promised Messiah.

It is the day of the Lord Joel describes in the first verse of the second chapter: "Blow ye the trumpet in Zion, and sound an alarm in my holy mountain: let all the inhabitants of the land tremble: for the day of the Lord cometh, for it is nigh at hand; A day of darkness and of gloominess, a day of clouds and of thick darkness, as the morning spread upon the mountains" (Joel 2:1, 2).

This was a great day, the most outstanding event in Israel's history. The people and their leaders were placed before the most important choice of all times!

Because the spiritual leaders failed to see "the things which" belonged to their own peace and to the peace of the people, the day of Christ became "a day of darkness and of gloominess, a day of clouds and of thick darkness." This day, however, ends as "the morning spread upon the mountains."

This is an expressive description of the day of the Lord as it appeared to the prophet Joel 700 years before it occurred. The morning was experienced by those who believed and received Christ. Those of Israel who rejected and crucified Him were given an extended time of grace for 40 years until 70 A.D. Then the cup of their iniquities was full, and the judgment came in the form of the destruction of Jerusalem.

The Roman general Titus, who laid waste Jerusalem with its temple, admitted that it must be God who permitted the judgment to pass upon this people. He also referred to the prediction made by Daniel and Jesus concerning the devastation of the city. When he first saw the fortifications of the city he considered it a superhuman undertaking to capture it.

Joel saw an invisible army storming the city. King David in his day had had that unseen force fighting for him as he fought against the Philistines for Israel's victory over Jerusalem. At that time he was told to wait until he would hear "the sound of a going in the tops of the mulberry trees"; then he should go to attack, "for then shall the Lord go out before thee, to smite the host of the Philistines" (II Sam. 5:24). It was apparently this same invisible army, which, according to Joel, fought against Israel and made the way for the Roman armies which came to destroy the city.

Josephus notes that Jerusalem had fallen in enemy hands five times but been completely destroyed only twice — by Nebuchadnezzar and the Babylonians and by the Romans.

Again I do not see why this necessarily refers to the fall of Jerusalem in 70 A.D.

The devastation was so terrible that the prophet exclaims: "For the day of the Lord is great and very terrible; and who can abide it?" (Joel 2:11).

When the Lord Himself is compelled to execute the chastisement of His people, then there is a day of the Lord with terrible consequences.

Not only Jerusalem was destroyed, but the people were scattered to all the lands of the earth. From that time Israel ceased to exist as a nation. They no longer had their own land, their own government, and a government seat.

### III

The promise to Abraham has always in a remarkable way tied Israel to the area of land God spoke of. The land itself, regardless of how it has changed hands, has never found a meaningful existence nor any rest, except when it has belonged to Israel. During David's and Solomon's time, when the country in its entirety was possessed by this people, there was a sense of unity and of a purposeful existence.

At other times it has been the battleground of foreign powers, and most of the time the land has been left uncultivated as a desert region. The country has never been what it should be without Israel, and this people has never been at peace nor existed under normal conditions away from their promised land. Down through the ages they have been meant for each other.

Ever since the dispersion of Israel from their land the people have had an indelible desire to return home. In the Jewish Passover rite there is an expression always voiced at the end of the Passover meal which marks the beginning of the week-long religious observance. It takes place at the conclusion of the meal, when the last drink is taken. As the cup is lifted they say what has been spoken in synagogues and Jewish homes all over the world for thousands of years: "Next year in Jerusalem!"

In this way the hope of returning to the land and to Jerusalem has been kept alive among this people. There have been sometimes weak and sometimes stronger efforts to make this a reality during the passing of the centuries.

In the meantime, the believing Jews, and often the large masses of this people, have called on God for mercy and help. This is exactly what the prophet Joel exhorted them to do. A wailing wall has not been found just in Jerusalem – we may say wherever this people has gathered for worship and also in many individual hearts such a wall has been present. Read what the prophet says:

"Turn ye even to me with all your heart, and with fasting, and with weeping, and with mourning:

"And rend your heart, and not your garments, and turn unto the Lord your God: for he is gracious and merciful, slow to anger, and of great kindness, and repenteth him of the evil.

"Who knoweth if he will return and repent, and leave a blessing behind him; even a meat offering and a drink offering unto the Lord your God?" (Joel 2:12-14).

With the 15th verse in the second chapter of Joel a new era has begun. The hope is beginning to find an expression in action. The Jews are beginning to gather for their return to the goal of their longings and desires. It is Zionism which is beginning to develop into a concrete form.

"Blow the trumpet in Zion, sanctify a fast, call a solemn assembly: gather the people, sanctify the congregation" (Joel 2:15, 16).

On August 29, 1897, the historical day arrived when the first congress of Zionism was opened in Basel, Switzerland. There were 196 delegates, and the chairman was the foremost promoter, Dr. Theodor Herzl. For the first time in more than eighteen hundred years a representative forum had been established, where ways and means for the return to Zion could be openly and officially discussed.

Shortly before that first Congress of Zionism, Dr. Herzl published his famous and pioneering volume: *The Jewish State.*

Zionism was an important part of Joel's prophecy, and it has been literally fulfilled in the minutest details.

But much remained to be done before Palestine would be opened to the Jews. There were years of taxing and sacrificial labor in the first Jewish colonies in the Holy Land. Then there were the negotiations with the great powers. This was especially true in the dealings with Turkey. Many disappointments and crushed expectations followed the efforts to return the land to the Jews. This was a literal fulfillment of Joel's prophecy, for, indeed, many an Israelite said: "Wherefore should they say among the people, Where is their God" (Joel 2:17). During those days of great conflict wonderful things happened.

Many supported the Zionist efforts. England, the United States, and France tried to politically influence the course of events in a positive way. But the great change came with World War I. Up to that time, all political moves had stranded. Now, however, a new world-remaking factor of such proportions entered that the leaders of the nations were forced by circumstances to become obedient servants.

On November 2, 1917, the British Foreign Minister Arthur James Balfour sent to Lord Rothschild the declaration of the British government that they supported the goals of the Zionist movement, namely that Palestine should be opened as a national home for the Jews.

Before this official declaration, involved negotiations had been carried on between the leaders of Zionism and Great Britain. One of the Zionist leaders, Dr. Chaim Weizmann, was able to establish communications with the leaders of the Arabs, Emir Faisal, who felt that the Jews and the Arabs should be able to live together in Syria and Palestine, for there was plenty of room. The area which is now known as Jordan originally belonged to Israel, and at the time of these negotiations had no more than about 300,000 Arab inhabitants.

The Balfour declaration, which has been considered one of the most remarkable acts of government, had filled both Jews and Christians with happy amazement. Not quite six weeks later there came some other just as exciting news: Jerusalem and Palestine had been taken by General Allenby and his British troops. The country, which for six centuries had been in the grip of Islam and for four hundred years had been under the dominion of Turkey, was now in the hands of Christians.

It was these tremendous events Joel had in mind when he wrote: "Then will the Lord be jealous for his land, and pity his people. . . . Fear not, O land; be glad and rejoice: for the Lord will do great things" (Joel 2:18, 21).

After the end of World War I the Jewish colony in Denmark held a banquet in Copenhagen. Speaker for the occasion was the Jewish philosopher and writer Georg Brandes, who at that time was a leading atheist and infidel in the Nordic lands. In his lecture he stated among other things that the just-concluded World War essentially was a loss to the whole world and to all fighting forces. The only positive result one could discover in this worldwide contest of power was that Palestine had been opened as a national home for the Jews.


IV

Over forty years from the founding of Zionism and about thirty years from December 11, 1918, when General Allenby marched into Jerusalem with his troops, had elapsed by the time the sovereign state of Israel was proclaimed on May 14, 1948, and the Jews officially took possession of their national home in Palestine. As earlier indicated, the country had then been under the Mohammedans for six hundred years and in the hands of the Turks for almost four centuries.

From the day the British army took Jerusalem until the day the country became a national home of the Jews, many conflicts and developments took place. Jordan was excluded from the area which the Balfour declaration promised to the Jews, the government under the mandate vacillated between Jewish and Arab interests, and also there were aggressive political and extremist forces within both camps, all of which issued in a violent tug-of-war by the time the Jewish state was born. The result was still that Israel received their land, even if it was with certain restrictions. Nevertheless, it had been accomplished through diplomacy, so that Israel never had to fire a single bullet to gain their end.

The prophetic description of how the country would blossom again begins with the 19th verse of the second chapter of Joel, and its fulfillment came long before 1948. The Zionist colonies opened a new era in the history of the country, but the real advancement came after the Turks had withdrawn, and the Jews took the leadership in politics, industry, and trade. This led to a total transformation.

The writer of these lines visited Palestine in 1922 for about seven months. The country was by and large a desert. There were a few large Jewish colonies. The Arabs used agricultural tools which seemed to date back to the time of the patriarchs, and their crops were deplorable. Industry was almost nonexistent, and the whole country was in a decadent state.

Since Israel took over the administration of the country there has been a great change in the development of the area; in fact, such a sudden transformation may never have seen its equal in the history of mankind.

Among the revenues the Turks had been demanding from the inhabitants of Palestine was a special tree tax; the people actually had to pay tax for every tree they possessed. To reduce the tax burden the people cut down their trees until the trees disappeared from the land. It is a well-known fact that there is a relationship between the prevalence of wooded areas and precipitation. Palestine consequently was not only without woods but to a great extent without rain. The land that once flowed with milk and honey had become waste because of mindless policies and devastating idleness.

In 1950, two years after Israel had been established, I visited the Holy Land once again. Intensive projects and works were under way, but not very much had been completed at that time. I visited Beersheba in the Negev Desert, but found only a new kibbutz. Apart from that the only attraction was Abraham's well, surrounded by sand dunes. In 1954 I returned again to Israel and saw the tremendous advances which had taken place. During a visit in 1961 I went down to Beersheba which by then had become a large city. We had lunch in an excellent restaurant. What a change! Now there is a city with a population of 69,500.

From Beersheba we continued our journey through the Negev district to the southern tip of the Dead Sea, and we found that this vast desert had been changed into fertile soil where rich crops of grain and vegetables were moving in the wind. What I saw reminded me of the lush fields of southern Sweden or the endless vegetable fields of California. This is, indeed, a literal fulfillment of the words of the prophet Isaiah: "The wilderness and the solitary place shall be glad for them; and the desert shall rejoice, and blossom as the rose" (Isa. 35:1).

This is what all tourists can view with their own eyes as they visit these areas.

Many wonder how it has been possible to construct irrigation systems and to cultivate these desert regions in such a short time. We can only explain it by pointing to God's good hand upon an energetic and industrious people.

"Behold, I will send you corn, and wine, and oil, and ye shall be satisfied therewith: and I will no more make you a reproach among the heathen. . . . Be glad then, ye children of Zion, and rejoice in the Lord your God: for he hath given you the former rain moderately, and he will cause to come down for you the rain, the former rain, and the latter rain in the first month. And the floors shall be full of wheat, and the fats shall overflow with wine and oil" (Joel 2:19, 23, 24).

Through Israel's initiative the forests have come back, and the rains have begun to fall more frequently than before. At my last visit to the land we experienced a real downpour in Jerusalem.

Israel's fruit and vegetables have made a place for themselves in the world's marketplaces for a number of years. In the year 1970 Sweden had fresh strawberries from Israel earlier than from any other country. These berries were generally held to be better looking and tasting than those from competitors which arrived at a later date.

All this information about how the country would flourish again is indicated in Joel's prophecy among the events which would precede the great outpouring of the Spirit.

In the midst of Joel's description of the blossoming forth of the country, which we are witnessing in our days, an abrupt interruption is inserted. It occurs in the twentieth verse of the second chapter where we read of a war which Israel has to fight.

"But I will remove far off from you the northern army, and will drive him into a land barren and desolate, with his face toward the east sea, and his hinder part toward the utmost sea, and his stink shall come up, and his ill savour shall come up, because he hath done great things" (Joel 2:20).

These are battles which Israel will fight while they are rebuilding their land. The recent alliance between Russia and Egypt could refer to the northern army. Does the Six-Day War in 1967 have a place in this dark image which is inserted in the otherwise bright prophetic picture?

The prophet Zechariah says, "And in that day will I make Jerusalem a burdensome stone for all people: all that burden themselves with it shall be cut in pieces, though all the people of the earth be gathered together against it" (Zech. 12:3).

A problem which more than anything has occupied the minds of the Israelis and filled them with disappointment has been the partition of the land. In the third chapter of Joel it is stated that God will judge the nations, because they "parted my land" (Joel 3:2). The kingdom of Jordan which was promised them in the Balfour declaration and especially the partition of Jerusalem have been constant sources of irritation for the Israelis.

In His prophecy concerning the destruction of Jerusalem, Jesus said, "And they shall . . . be led away captive into all nations; and Jerusalem shall be trodden down of the Gentiles, until the times of the Gentiles be fulfilled" (Luke 21:24).

Christians have centered much of their attention on this prediction. Many have had the opinion that because Israel rejected Christ as their Messiah they lost their mission of being the vehicles of the divine revelation, and with this Israel's time came to an end, and the times of the Gentiles began. The Christian church of called-out-ones from the Gentiles then became the vehicle of the divine revelation. But now since Jerusalem no longer is ruled by a foreign power, and Israel possesses the whole city, the Jewish people has again a prominent place in God's plan of salvation. God is again counting with His Old Covenant people.

This must not be interpreted to mean that God will not continue to deal with and use His church. Many Scriptures certainly support His unending interest in the church. The prophecy which Jesus uttered, as indicated above, was, however, closely tied to Israel as a nation. Israel was to return to their land, and the entire city of Jerusalem was to be surrendered to them; and these events would mark the beginning of a new era. Israel would again find their place in God's original plan. This is exactly where we are since the June war of 1967.

This present situation is spoken of by the God of Israel through Joel in the following words: "And my people shall never be ashamed. And ye shall know that I am in the midst of Israel, and that I am the Lord your God, and none else: and my people shall never be ashamed" (Joel 2:26, 27).

Israel has experienced the fulfillment of the prophetic word, and they are back in their land. God has again incorporated them in His original plan for them as a people.

Immediately after this follows the 28th verse with its message: "And it shall come to pass afterward, that I will pour out my spirit upon all flesh." In this, of course, Israel is included also, and we are already now seeing evidences of this outpouring of the Spirit in many parts of the world.

## V

In conjunction with what is happening in and around Israel at the present, God will pour out His Spirit upon all flesh — that includes the Jewish people. By the Spirit of the Lord, Zechariah says, "I will pour upon the house of David, and upon the inhabitants of Jerusalem, the spirit of grace and of supplications: and they shall look upon me whom they have pierced" (Zech. 12:10).

God will choose people whom He may fill with His Spirit and will use them in a revival among His people Israel. Already in that modern state men have appeared on the scene who remind us of the Old Testament prophets. They expound the writings of Moses and the prophets and interpret predictions regarding Israel's future. They have gained the confidence of the people and are highly regarded in all sections of society. A movement, much reminiscent of the prophetism of this nation's old history, seems to be under way.

It is very likely that the outpouring of the Holy Spirit in Israel will begin in this way. The same God and the same Spirit who moved on the first Day of Pentecost almost two thousand years ago in Jerusalem is at work today. At that time, primarily Jews from all over the then known world opened their hearts and received the message concerning their crucified and risen Messiah. A new outpouring of the Spirit will be the means whereby the majority of the Jewish people will believe in Christ as their true Messiah.

The very purpose of the Holy Spirit's ministry is to open the eyes of Israel and of the Gentile world so that they may see that Christ is the Messiah and the Lord of this world. This is a movement which with the last days' outpouring of the Spirit will come parallel to Antichrist's powerful efforts to conquer the world.

Just as we see in Israel clear signs in this direction, we can see in the rest of the world mighty manifestations of a new revival. It is especially remarkable that many Christians, who have been strangers to the truths concerning the baptism in the Spirit and the gifts of the Spirit, in ever-increasing numbers have been awakened to reality of these spiritual riches.

Priests and ministers revise their concepts, and churches with their boards realize how futile it is to carry on the work of the Gospel unless the Holy Spirit comes to rule in His mighty power. Repeatedly we hear of clergymen who stand up before their churches making the most gripping confessions. They have discovered that they have preached a Gospel, the power of which they never really understood. Their preaching has in the main been confined to outward works of salvation, to Christian behavior, but they have never experienced nor grasped the fullness of the power of God unto salvation that the Gospel really is. But now this side of Christianity has been brought to their attention. They have understood that it is only by the Holy Spirit that Christ and His work can be made alive to the individual, to the church, and to the world.

With the change in attitude among preachers and pastors almost everything has been changed. This is one of the reasons why we have witnessed such amazing things in the last few years. Ministers and priests have been baptized in the Holy Spirit — and thousands of laymen with them.

In some instances the churches have dismissed their pastor because he received the baptism in the Holy Spirit. But this has only forced him into other areas to preach his message, and the movement has thus been further spread. In the meantime the outpouring of the Spirit continued in the congregation he was forced to leave. This has been the situation in thousands of places around the world.

The hunger and thirst for God controls a spiritual movement, such as we are speaking of, and no human hand, however strong it may be, can hold the reins.

The same movement is sweeping the large worldwide church organizations and the smaller Protestant church bodies alike. In one of the cities of California, where I am residing as I write these lines, a Baptist church has had an experience which has caused much excitement.

The pastor of this particular church has been a deliberate, and no doubt, sincere enemy of the Pentecostal revival. He has preached against it, and members who received the Holy Spirit were told to leave the church. Many of the leaders and the members in general shared his attitude.

Then some time ago one of the more important leaders of the church, a medical doctor, rose to his feet in a service and testified, saying that he had been baptized in the Holy Spirit and spoken in tongues. He further stated that he had opposed the Pentecostal experience, and that he had spoken against the charismatic movement, but now he had a different view on these matters. Tears coursing down his cheeks, he shared this testimony with the congregation, and it caused quite a stirring among the listeners in the church which was full of people.

The result is that the pastor of this church has changed his attitude and is now preaching the necessity of the Baptism in the Holy Spirit. In his church bulletin he writes that the Spirit must have free course in the life of the individual and of the church. He urges his people to pray that the Spirit may convict all of this truth, and that the things of the Spirit may be more real to the pastor, the deacons, the choir and all who serve the church in any way. In this manner a church which once hindered an outpouring of the Spirit now is a means of spreading it, and all who know what has happened are indeed amazed.

These events, *per se,* are remarkable, but the most important thing about them is what they promise for the future. This is a testimony of what is going to happen in the churches on a much larger scale.

We are also witnessing other inspiring developments in that many preachers who experience the baptism in the Holy Spirit, contrary to all expectations, are accepted by their ecclesiastical superiors and by their churches. By way of example, let me mention a Roman Catholic parish in California, where recently one of the priests received the baptism. His testimony is very interesting.

After he received the baptism in the Holy Spirit he was to preach in one service and was expected to speak on the prescribed text for that day. When he came to the service he informed the parish priest that he through the Holy Spirit had received a message which was not centered around the text for the day, and then he asked, "What shall I do?"

"Deliver the message you received," said the priest in charge. He did so, and his message was recorded. I have had the opportunity to listen to it and can testify that it is one of the most stirring messages I have ever heard. It is a concise, pithy and touching address on a question directed to Christianity at large: "What have you done with my Son's church?"

It is a prophetic message with judgment upon the church which goes through bones and marrow. At the same time, the style is so beautiful that someone remarked, "No contemporary poet could have chosen a more eloquent expression."

This priest has been given freedom to continue to deliver the messages he receives through the Spirit. This has brought revival to young and old. On the tape on which I heard him speak, he tells of a group of teenagers, eleven of them, who gathered for prayer. Many of them have been baptized in the Holy Spirit. Among these young people, and through them, remarkable healings have taken place. The priest himself has also been an instrument used in bringing outstanding healings and miracles. This is what is going on in numerous large church organizations throughout the world.

There are also many evidences of the Spirit being

outpoured upon people who do not even confess to be Christians. One of my sons in California told me about the following incident which took place when I visited him in the spring of 1970.

A Christian foreman of a large company was calling on various customers to make sure that the services rendered by his company employees were satisfactory. After a brief conversation about various business matters, the owner of one corporation said to this foreman:

"Step into my office. I have something important I want to talk to you about."

Once in the office he continued his conversation with the Christian visitor: "You speak of giving your hearts to Jesus and surrendering your lives to God. What do you really mean with these expressions? There are many who would be interested in knowing more about these things.

"Would it be possible for you who know a lot about such matters to gather with some of the rest of us and give us an opportunity to ask questions? You could really help us with our problems. Your boss has bought a restaurant here in the city. Do you suppose he would let some of us businessmen gather there for some informal meetings?"

The result of this conversation is that at 6:30 A.M. once a week a large group of businessmen, most of them not committed Christians, gathers in that restaurant for Bible reading and prayer.

Isn't it likely that this kind of development is the result of an outpouring of the Spirit upon all flesh?

# III

# *The Crisis Of The Churches*

## THE CRISIS OF THE CHURCH DENOMINATIONS

It is apparent in our days that people are getting tired of large organizations and church councils. This is probably a tendency which will be observed not only in the religious world but also in the secular. Cooperation and fellowship have their place in both spiritual and secular contexts, but this has been carried a little too far. The reaction is apparently coming and seems to be on the way already.

If we concentrate on our observations from the religious activities in our time we note a movement which tends toward less rigid forms. This tendency is probably quite general and can be noticed more or less in all countries. In the United States where religion has a prominent place in the public life and always is treated with respect, this question is under discussion in both the religious and secular press.

The ecclesiastical denominations have lost the authority they once had, it is felt. Both the Catholic church and Protestant denominations are passing through a crisis of rather remarkable proportions.

In the Catholic church many priests rebel against practices which have been considered irrevocable. They protest against celibacy and many leave the priesthood. They refuse to submit to the church's questionable doctrines concerning morality and are demanding personal freedom of conscience.

Many nuns are protesting against the old system with its isolation behind cloistered walls and demand freedom and possibilities to serve in a more natural and practical way.

There is also a spiritual movement within the Catholic church. Many of their members are gathering in simple cottage meetings, where they study the Bible and pray. Many of them have been baptized in the Holy Spirit. Among these are a number of priests. At one Catholic university in Indiana a renewal has been going on for some time among both students and professors.

Pope John XXIII in several ways softened the rigidity of the Roman Catholic Church's doctrines, but Paul VI is considered more conservative.

The movement which now is occurring within and approaching Roman Catholicism from several directions cannot be stopped by the hierarchy interested in preserving man's traditions. Catholicism will have to choose between the Word of God or traditions of men.

Also within the Protestant churches there is a crisis now in the U.S. This means, in many instances, to try to avoid the crisis the churches vary old programs; but they are just a little more strained and even less effective than before. Everything is apparently moving toward a point where a great change will take place within the church world.

This entire crisis can, without a doubt, be described as a battle between collectivism and individualism. These are two values in human relationships which are both perfectly legitimate. Their value, however, depends in the highest degree upon the fact that each knows its own limitations. The great injustices or delusions in the world often had their basis in the fact that either one of these two potentates grabbed too much space at the expense of the other.

It is around this point that the tug of war has been fought in the battle between different political social groups. It is also in this area that the spiritual revivals have caused the greatest crises. The ecclesiastical unity in such contests has always had to yield to the standpoint taken by individuals and to justified groupings. It is remarkable also that individuals taking a position on a personal basis and the protests of small groups against the misdirected attitudes of the large entities in the end most likely will trigger this crisis. The goal awaiting the religious movement in the world, whether there is awareness of it or not, is a personal Christianity with a spiritual fellowship which will be confined to smaller entities.

This is what has been experienced in several countries already. Several of the South American countries are passing through such a spiritual crisis. There Catholicism to a great extent has lost its hold on the people. It is primarily the Pentecostal revival in countries like Brazil and Chile which has given Protestantism the strong spiritual lead it enjoys.

In Europe where many Protestant churches function as national churches, the situation is much the same as in the so-called Catholic nations. The influence they used to have through their privileged position has disappeared to a great extent. The Lutheran Church in Sweden, for instance, is just a shadow of what it once was. It has been a real backbone of Christian influence at home, at school and in the public life, but the church has lost this position. At one time the church exerted influence upon the state and the people, but now the state through the government and "Riksdag" has robbed her of the most vital rights, even in wholly spiritual matters.

The free churches (churches other than the state church in Sweden) are experiencing a strong decline. Their membership during the last few years has been decimated in a catastrophic way. The Sociological Institute of Stockholm has already predicted the year each one of these denominations will cease to exist. The causes of these conditions are discouraging, and they affect a work which has been carried on for years through great sacrifices, but the present trend is nevertheless a fact.

What has been stated can be applied to conditions all over the world. In the totalitarian countries the churches have been crushed. In the Soviet Union a sort of fake organization of free churches is permitted which apparently serves two purposes: to give the world the impression that Russians enjoy freedom of religion, and then that the atheistic regime may have the Christian work under its control. It is known that they have tools who serve the Communist system by submitting their work to the pattern laid out by the party, and they remain loyal to this regime. Real Christianity, however, exists in Russia outside the totalitarian restrictions.

Except for a few minor details the conditions are the same in Red China and other Communist countries. The churches and their organizations as the missionaries built them are gone. The Christianity which remains is primarily very personal in character. They are limited to a spiritual experience which makes the believer dependent (wholly) upon God and direct communication with the eternal world. Christian fellowship under such circumstances is limited to meetings of small groups.

Everything seems to point to a new orientation for Christian work. The super-organization of the churches in itself is a condition calling for simplification. There is a need for streamlining in order to gain greater freedom and to reduce the great cost of denominational administration.

The realism which is gripping the masses of Christians cannot be satisfied by the organizational and ceremonial programs which the churches offer. The people want something other than attractive religious forms and platitudes. They desire to get in touch with spiritual and eternal realities. A simple testimony from a person who has experienced what he is talking about is preferred, and so is also a Bible study which strengthens the life of faith; this is much better than carefully thought out and intellectual sermons.

The beautiful churches with their expensive refinements tend to make a negative impression on people who are spiritually hungry. They prefer the simplest meeting place or the humblest home for their gatherings.

The Christian church is about to be forced back to the effective methods of the early church by inside, as well as external, forces.

# ADVANCE IN SPITE OF DECLINE

Success is not always proof of rightness. Evil, and sometimes rather inconsequential works of man, can be successful depending upon various conditions and circumstances. But Jesus pointed to a sure sign which shows that Christianity is intrinsically good and that its success is a blessing to humanity.

The proof Jesus advanced was that of its fruit. He said, that which bears good fruit must be good. "Do men gather grapes of thorns, or figs of thistles? Even so every good tree bringeth forth good fruit; but a corrupt tree bringeth forth evil fruit. . . . " (Matt. 7:16-20).

Christianity has demonstrated that it bears good fruit where it has had an opportunity to show its power. Its life-transforming salvation experience is a tangible reality which no sensible person can deny. Its mission Jesus expressed in the condensed, well-known words: "For the Son of man is come to seek and to save that which was lost" (Luke 19:10). Where this program has been put into effect by representatives of Christianity, good and rich fruits which always accompany living Christianity are harvested.

The spiritual wealth which the Christian experience provides is, of course, the first and most important fruit of this tree of life. Christianity, however, has given humanity many material blessings of inestimable value. Think of how Christianity has brought education, medical care, and social relief to many parts of the world. Pay special attention to the Christian influence upon lawmaking, justice, and norms of personal behavior. The success of Christianity leads to the success of the good!

The decline in membership in the Christian denominations is not necessarily any evidence that Christianity is declining. Neither is the decreasing enrollment at seminaries and Bible schools a proof of Christian decline. Some have made the mistake of saying that Christian churches equal Christianity. Then it has been stated that the clergy of different times constituted the true representation of Christ's cause upon earth. But it has often been evident that Christianity's real representatives were found outside the recognized clergy and outside the churches which thought they were the best and indisputable representatives of Christianity. Therefore, a decrease in denominational membership does not necessarily mean a decline of living Christianity.

We would go too far in our differentiation if we were to say that denominations and Christianity are altogether different concepts. Of course, Christianity is found within all Christian denominations, and in many instances much of the real kind. Still it would be wrong to say that these denominations represent Christianity.

Jesus said: "Woman, believe me, the hour cometh, when ye shall neither in this mountain, nor yet at Jerusalem, worship the Father. . . . But the hour cometh, and now is, when the true worshippers shall worship the Father in spirit and in truth" (John 4:21, 23).

Christianity is a spiritual religion where neither temples, ceremonies, clergy, nor organizations are necessary for man's fellowship with God. Every person in this Gospel age can have fellowship with God without these intermediaries. The existence of denominations is not a deciding factor in the matter of Christianity's victory in the world. Christianity's success was never greater than **before** the time of Christian denominations!

Temporary defeats among Christians are not decisive relative to the final victory of Christianity. The reverses which the cause of Christianity suffers through resistance and attacks from the outside and through weaknesses within cannot hinder its victory in the world.

Heresies, wrong methods, and sin can cause suffering and delay the success but never hinder the final victory. Christianity is a divine phenomenon, and one can no more stop it than the rising of the sun at the appointed time. However dark the night, nothing can stop the dawn and light of the morning. Neither can any forces of darkness, regardless of how formidable they may be, hinder the Son of Rightousness to rise "with healing in his wings."

Christianity's advance and final victory is based on facts beyond the reach of human control and human influence. Its resources are divine. He who created the universe with its many still unexplored secrets and who still upholds it "by the word of his power" is the One who with all His resourcefulness leads the cause of Christ. That He decided to use weak human beings as His instruments to serve His great cause is an expression of His superior way of confounding the wisdom of this world. "Because the foolishness of God is wiser than men; and the weakness of God is stronger than men" (I Cor. 1:25).

He uses weak human instruments as wires which conduct the divine power. When the children of this world and materialistic Christians discover the weakness of these conductors, they prophesy Christianity's collapse.

At the appearing of Christianity the human element revealed a tremendous weakness. It came in the form of a carpenter surrounded by rumors of unbelievable events which placed Jesus and His closest companions in the center of a remarkable controversy. The virgin birth, His humble descent, His lack of formal education at the institutions of learning of that day, and His opposition to the accepted religious system erected a wall against His message. The work He accomplished, through the radiance from His pure and noble personality, His glorious preaching, and His powerful miracles and signs, soon reached its climax; but quicker yet came the reverses which looked more like a total failure.

The large throngs left Him as soon as He began to speak about His suffering and death. Even the twelve whom He had chosen to be His apostles forsook Him and fled. Prior to this, however, one of them sold Him to His enemies for thirty pieces of silver, and at His public trial, the most prominent one denied his discipleship three times and swore that he did not know Him. Humanly speaking, the beginning of Christianity ended with its founder, alone and forsaken by

God and by man, hanging on a cross between two thieves.

This was the collapse of Christianity at the very start, as His enemies and many of the believing Jews saw it. They did not see God's plan of salvation which was behind this event that superficially seemed so discouraging. What appeared to be the greatest defeat, however, was the greatest victory the cause of God ever won! Calvary's victory is *the* victory above all others!

# *Victorious Faith—*
# *Our Guiding Star*

A journalist some time ago confronted me with a question concerning Christianity's prospects for victory. He did this in such a way that I began to give more and more thought to it. His question was backed by reliable and well-supported arguments and has created a real need within me to find a satisfying answer.

He argued as follows:

"You know that Christianity does not keep pace with the population increase in the world. Many more people are born than the number of new converts and new members added to the Christian churches. You are also aware of the fact that all the religious denominations in Sweden are retrogressing, and that the same conditions exist in other parts of the world.

"You also know that strong forces are on foot in our country and in other lands to extinguish Christianity by legal and political action. You also know that some of our contemporary political tactics are aimed at undermining the morality of the nations which are historically known as the torchbearers of Christian democracy. This applies especially to nations such as England, the United States, and the Scandinavian countries.

"You know that even within the Christian churches there are negative forces undermining verities which have been the pillars of Christian experience, Christian work, and Christian culture. Amongst these you find those who proclaim that God is different from what He is described to be in the Bible, and prominent Christians disseminate such teachings through literature and press.

"You are aware of this; with these observations in view, do you still believe that Christianity will be victorious?"

This, then, was the question of the journalist.

Ever since I was first questioned in this manner, I have wrestled with the problem, and (gradually) I have come to realize that I must find an answer. My many years of studying the Scriptures, history, the people, and the conditions in the world which have existed during my long and extensive experience, have helped to provide an answer. Separated from the demanding pastoral duties of the church, I have had more time for studies and travels in different countries, and this has given me a wider view of the question than I have had before. Not least has this been true about my latest visit in South America, where I had the opportunity to see and study the most successful contemporary Christian movements, and these observations help, indeed, to find an answer to this question which I consider the most important of our day.

## FAITH IN VICTORY

Many years ago I had a surprise visit by the well-known, and at that time very influential, Foreign Missions Secretary of the Mission Covenant Church in Sweden, the Rev. Jakob Lundahl. He had returned from the Missions Conference in Jerusalem 1928, one of the important conclaves of world missions. There the very elite and most prominent of missions leaders had been gathered.

The many difficulties, which since then have beset Christian missions endeavors, were at that time already foreshadowed in various parts of the world. Not long after this conference, China was closed to missionary work. The nationalistic movements in missions lands were early indications that the foreign missionary program would have to undergo great changes.

Pastor Lundahl was a prominent man, not only within his

own denomination, but highly respected among all Christians in and outside of Sweden. He was looked upon as an outstanding foreign missions authority. He was also a man with a heart on fire for the cause of Christ, and he was a man who had an impressive knowledge of missions. We had become personal friends and contacted each other occasionally. He was a warmhearted Bible believer and had partaken of the Pentecostal experience, although he was not an official member of the Pentecostal movement.

At the time of this mentioned visit he spoke of the conference which he had attended and now had returned from. He shared with me his impressions. The conference was a magnificent manifestation of the vast scope of missions, its resources and results. In spite of this he did not try to hide a certain disappointment over what he had heard and seen during the conference.

I cannot repeat his words verbatim, but the general concepts have often passed through my memory. They registered in my consciousness, marking one of the soul-shaking instances when I met the question of the "to be or not to be" of Christianity. Therefore, I have never been able to forget the unexpected but much appreciated visit, and what Jakob Lundahl said at that time.

He spoke of the extraordinary resources at the disposal of Christian missions today and of possibilities of entering open doors. Thoroughgoing reports had made this clear at the conference. He enumerated funds, educational institutions, health programs, and an impressive staff ready and prepared for the various tasks.

"But," he said, "I missed something very essential."

His voice vibrated with emotion as he said, "**I missed a conquering faith.**"

On the way home he had meditated over this and decided to see me in order to share his observations.

"In the Pentecostal movement there are many weaknesses and much which is far from perfect," he said, "but you have something which many denominations and associations lack, and that is CONQUERING FAITH. It is this faith which must extend and spread among all Christians. Without this faith the Christian church and its missionary program can never lead the cause of Christ to victory.

"The problems and the difficulties Christianity and its outreach meet, not least in our day, are superhuman and can never be solved with mere human means. Faith in God, which counts with supernatural and divine power, alone is able to provide such conquering faith."

Approximately, such were the words of the good and God-fearing missions leader.

This memorable visit was concluded with prayer and a tender and heart-warming admonition to God's Spirit-filled people to continue to fight for CONQUERING FAITH.

The greatest risk in the kingdom of God has always been that people may choose other ways than those of living faith. In regard to man's fellowship with God, faith is the only way. Never has anyone found a way to God by any other means. The wavelengths of knowledge, feeling, and imagination have been tried, but always with the same negative result. For the advancement of the work of God in the world, man has tried these side-paths, but never with the expected results.

It is faith in God which unites man with Him and the eternal divine resources. The victorious battle against evil has always been fought by faith, and on that level it must be fought until the final victory is won.

In the parable of the widow and the unjust judge, Jesus gave us an exposure of a time filled with temptations which His followers were to encounter toward the end of the Gospel age. This is where He speaks of enduring prayer as the outward and visible means whereby righteousness shall conquer. He explains, however, that this will depend on whether at that time there is found such faith as will be victorious. It was the widow's faith in success for her cause which gave her courage to continue when others might have grown weary.

It is this question Jesus directs to the Christians of the last days: will He find such faith when He comes, a faith which, firm as a rock, conquers all obstacles? Though God might "bear long with them" before He avenges His elect, this kind of faith will not be shaken. It endures until divine justice prevails.

Jesus raises the question as to whether this faith will be found when He comes. There are those who have interpreted these words of Jesus to mean that this faith will not be found when He returns. But Jesus never said this. He leaves the answer to this question with the people of faith. You and I, or those who will be living at the time Jesus has in mind in this parable, will answer that question of the Savior.

He does affirm, however, that God will avenge His people and the cause they fight for. The calm assurance of Jesus is "I tell you that he will avenge them speedily" (Luke 18:8). This is the solemn assurance Jesus gave concerning the final victory of Christianity.

What faith in victory means to a nation and its troops in time of war, our contemporary strategists understand and take advantage of to the nth degree. We have been told about the extraordinary steps which were taken in the last world wars to create this faith in victory among the troops. At the same time enormous efforts were made to infiltrate amongst the enemy troops — a lack of confidence in their leadership, in their national resources, and in final victory. One realized that the enemy's loss of faith in victory was a more important factor in the final defeat than the weapons used against him.

The most deplorable situation is when someone with every possibility for victory imagines that defeat is inevitable. In that way, discouraged and defeated in spirit, he goes against the enemy.

Paul in all of his varied experiences describes the Christian's attitude toward the triumphant end of Christ's work in a shout of jubilation:

"Now thanks be unto God, which always causeth us to triumph in Christ, and maketh manifest the savour of His knowledge by us in every place" (II Cor. 2:14).

Christian faith builds on realities. We don't just believe, but we have reality factors upon which we build our conquering faith. In fact, this faith is built upon realities more substantial and concrete than any material things.

Moshe Dayan, the defense minister in Israel, some time back was asked how a small nation with limited resources can hope to win in a military contest with far superior enemy forces.

It is possible, he held, if the weaker contestant has weapons which the stronger enemy does not possess, and if he uses other methods than the enemy.

What is needed today is that the church begin to believe in and put to use the superior weapons and methods which God has given to her. But the great mistake in Christianity today is that all kinds of human things have been introduced into its spiritual life and ministry. In many instances the church has overlooked the spiritual armor and the divine weapons which were so generously given to the early Christian church. There are even those who have felt that all kinds of human efforts are acceptable substitutes for this divine armor. This is the explanation of the present, prevailing spiritual condition.

The means God can use in leading people to an experience of salvation and in bringing about the victory in His kingdom are so many and so varied that they cannot be cataloged. The simplest and least expected means and events can be cause of a spiritual conversion. The Holy Spirit can speak to the heart of man, convict of sin, and guide to a living faith in Jesus through instruments and circumstances which no one ever would have thought possible.

There are, however, some weapons which are generally used in bringing the cause of Christ to victory.

My intention, at this point, is just briefly to refer to the armor and the weapons which still belong to the Christian church. Then throughout this volume my purpose will be to repeatedly return our attention to the mighty arsenal God has placed at the disposition of His people. And this includes offensive as well as defensive weapons the like of which our enemy does not possess.

We have first the Gospel. Our adversaries have their propaganda, and they have tremendous resources for distributing it. But the Gospel has an inherent divine power the like of which its enemies can not claim.

There is healing power in the Gospel. Torn and fragmented human lives, wounded and smarting consciences, and sick and suffering bodies are made whole. It is the divine power which accompanies the Gospel of Jesus that meets the crying needs for help present in every age and among all peoples.

Prayer is also one of the powerful weapons by which the church and the individual Christian can attain remarkable results. It is a long-range weapon, and with it the praying man can reach any place on earth, even the most remote and hidden areas. There are millions of examples of the tremendous power of prayer. When a believing Christian, or a group of such Christians, devote themselves to fervent and persevering prayer one can rest assured that something will happen. Prayer is an irresistible force.

The most powerful and most decisive tools God has given His church are the human instruments whom He calls and fits for service in His kingdom.

Some years ago an American general made a statement which I have never been able to forget. He said that we speak of and invent new weapons, and we place great emphasis on the military equipment, but we hear very little about the personnel and the importance of the men in the armed forces. Still it is upon them that everything depends. Without capable people who can use the weapons in the right way we get nowhere regardless of how modern and perfected our war implements may be.

The most important and most decisive weapons God equips and uses are people who are willing to place themselves at His disposal.

What was one of the most important measures Jesus took in order to promulgate His message and to offer the world the opportunity to partake of His salvation? He selected human instruments, prepared them, and equipped them for the task. The ones He chose were not perfect people. They were "unlearned and ignorant men" (Acts 4:13), but they were dedicated. He caused them to go through purifying fires as they walked with Him during His short period of ministry. They were tempted and suffered defeats, such as in the events surrounding the crucifixion. But He did not stop with this. He met them after His resurrection and led them back to a living faith in Himself and in the cause He had left with them. Finally He outfitted them with a mighty baptism in the Holy Spirit.

In this manner they were prepared and equipped with divine power and went out to win victories greater than they had ever imagined.

The very same thing will happen again as humanity shall experience the outpouring of the Holy Spirit upon all flesh in conjunction with the last-day events and the second coming of Jesus.

The most powerful weapon against sin and the evil in the world is the unyielding desire for God which is laid down in the mind of man. Man's conscience, his demands for purity, his consciousness of eternity, and the thought of corruption never leave him. This desire for God is so great among men that God will always have instruments willing to be placed at His disposal. In the final analysis, this guarantees the victory of Christ in the world.

This will also play the leading role in the great outpouring of the Spirit upon all flesh.

# V

# The Spiritual Equipment

## The Gifts of the Spirit

When rationalism reduced religion to a concern of the intellect only, it simplified a many-sided and complicated problem and made it a narrow and confined phenomenon. There are, however, many aspects, other than the intellectual which are of foremost importance in man's relationship to God. Christianity's advantage in the battle against evil can be seen in its supernatural resources.

Remove the religion of Jesus to the intellectual level and it will have many enemies opposing with formidable strength. On the other hand, however, let it appear in its supernatural armor, and, according to Christ's promise, "the gates of hell shall not prevail against it" (Matt. 16:18).

The religious element in man does not embrace just the intellect; no, it embraces the entire world of the mind, including intellect, will, emotions and all their ramifications. Religion touches the entire man — spirit, soul, and body. The entire human being is influenced by God and His Gospel. When man reacts, be it negatively or positively, he does so not just with his intellect but with this entire being. His will and emotions are involved to a very great extent.

This is also strongly underlined by the presentation of Christianity which Jesus and His apostles made. We have witnessed, however, how the spiritual power with which Christianity was endued in apostolic days has been replaced with strictly human ability and human means. The disastrous results speak for themselves. We are left with a Christianity in word but not in power.

The very last words of Jesus, before His ascension, made it clear that the baptism in the Holy Spirit would be the equipment which would make them efficient witnesses for Him. The great mission which had been entrusted to them was to disciple all nations, and the baptism in the Holy Spirit was the only equipment He promised them. If they received this free gift, as well as the gifts of the Spirit which follow this initial experience, then they would be properly equipped for their great task.

All Christians have been commissioned to win their fellow-men for God. Therefore, every Christian needs to be spiritually equipped for this task.

Whoever so will has access to the gifts which the Spirit bestows. These are of such a nature that they constitute the best equipment for the above-mentioned commission. The apostle Paul enumerated these gifts: "For to one is given by the Spirit the word of wisdom; to another the word of knowledge by the same Spirit; to another faith by the same Spirit; to another the gifts of healing by the same Spirit; to another the working of miracles; to another prophecy; to another discerning of spirits; to another divers kinds of tongues; to another the interpretation of tongues" (I Cor. 12:8-10).

Added to the armor of the baptism in the Holy Spirit we have in these gifts an arsenal of weapons which are intended to be used for the task of winning men and women to God.

Much wisdom is needed for this mission. This is apparently the reason why this gift, the gift of the word of wisdom, is first mentioned.

Just think of how much wisdom is needed to approach, in a right way, ones we desire to win. As individuals, whether in the home, at work, at school, or as leaders, we need wisdom to represent Christ in a right way.

More than anyone else the preacher of the Gospel needs it. When many of these gifts are present with a preacher, marvelous results can be accomplished. When a minister has the gifts of the word of wisdom, the word of knowledge, and prophecy, speaking in tongues, interpretation of tongues, discerning of spirits, he is well-equipped for his work. Add to these the gifts of faith, healing, and miracles.

It was because the Christians of the first centuries had these qualifications that they were able to influence the age in which they lived to such a great extent. Through the supernatural power which was revealed in their ministry, the banner of the cross was raised all over the then known world, and they finally gained control over the Roman Empire. It was not "cunningly devised fables" and human book-learning which achieved this. The apostle Paul gives an account of the contents in his preaching and in that of his contemporary Christians: "We speak . . . as it is written. Eye hath not seen, nor ear heard, neither have entered into the heart of man, the things which God hath prepared for them that love Him. But God hath revealed them unto us by His Spirit; for the Spirit searcheth all things, yea, the deep things of God" (I Cor. 2:7-10).

How can a person possibly produce such preaching without the equipment of the Baptism in the Holy Spirit and the gifts of the Spirit?

The gift of the word of wisdom is given to aid our understanding. Jesus said: "Ye shall know the truth, and the truth shall make you free" (John 8:32). The gift of the word of wisdom enables us not only to understand the truth but to speak the Word of God so that our listeners understand. The speaker is capable of expounding the deepest divine truths in a simple and easily understandable way. By the Spirit of revelation he is led to deal with just the kind of problems the listeners are wrestling with. This makes the preaching interesting and gripping. When questions are answered, people find release; and this is often a great help in bringing salvation to the unconverted and spiritual nourishment and times of refreshing to God's people.

In order that the speaker should choose the right particular portion of knowledge the listeners need, God has given the gift of the word of knowledge. The knowledge comes by reading the Holy Scriptures. Thus it is necessary to know the contents of the Bible. One of the effects of the Spirit is a love for the Word. The word of knowledge consists of speaking words of knowledge. This is an enablement to use the Scriptures correctly in convincing men of the divine truth. Stephen's speech which is recorded in Acts 7 is a typical example of the word of knowledge in operation. He demonstrates, with references to Israel's history, how God again and again sought this people, but they always resisted God — even as on this occasion.

In the word of knowledge is also a love for the written revelation, a desire to search its depths and to understand the right relationship between the contents of various Scriptures and in a correct and faithful way to use this knowledge of the Word. How important that this gift is operative in order to give God's people a right knowledge in the Holy Scriptures.

Faith finds a field of action in just about every direction in our Christian work. It is this power which must support and carry the preaching. To the extent that this is done the preaching will be alive and fruitbearing in all circumstances. Faith is spoken of as one of the gifts of the Spirit. This is miracle-working faith. If such faith is needed anywhere, it certainly is in our labors for the salvation of men and women. Jesus gave an eloquent illustration of the place of faith in our spiritual sowing.

"And he said, So is the kingdom of God, as if a man should cast seed into the ground; And should sleep, and rise night and day, and the seed should spring and grow up, he knoweth not how. For the earth bringeth forth fruit of herself; first the blade, then the ear, after that the full corn in the ear. But when the fruit is brought forth, immediately he putteth in the sickle, because the harvest is come" (Mark 4:26-29).

He who would reap must have faith in that which is mysterious, in the power of growth, and in the reality of that which is supernatural: "The seed should spring and grow up, he knoweth not how." The process is mysterious, and the human responsibility is simply to have faith; one must believe in God, believe in the soil which represents the people with whom we work; one must have faith in the seed, which is the Word of God which we sow, and one must believe that the labors will bring fruit. If wonder-working faith is needed anywhere it is in our evangelistic outreach.

The preaching or the sowing should also create faith, for "faith comes by preaching and preaching comes through the power of Christ's word" (Rom. 10:17, direct translation from Swedish). There is much preaching which creates problems instead of solving them and raises questions instead of giving answers. Such preaching is void of the revelation of the Spirit. A sermon inspired by the Holy Spirit helps the listeners with the difficulties of life, and solves problems which may seem without solution as far as human wisdom is concerned. It is in this area that the Bible gives much knowledge and many examples.

The gifts of healing the sick also belong to the equipment of the preacher. We know what a tremendous complement this was to the preaching of Christ and the apostles.

These gifts have also brought wonderful blessings in our days, as we have seen. They are given to various people. Some seem to manifest them in a small degree, while others in a much greater. Through sound and continuous instruction God's people will believe these truths, and it will be quite natural for them to go to God also with their physical needs. This is a message which answers a great need in our days.

Add to these gifts the working of miracles and you have a powerful equipment for the ministry, whether it be to win people by personal evangelism or by proclaiming the Gospel to large audiences.

All who know the Bible know how much such divine interventions in human lives have meant to the work of God in the past. It is at this point that rationalism has concentrated its resistance; the object is to cull out the supernatural in Christianity. The supernatural, however, is the secret weapon against which rational religion has no adequate weapon.

The gifts of the Holy Spirit are given to members of the congregation as well as to the pastor. By the working together between pastor and members a new vitality and interest is developed in the local church.

## THE FRUIT OF THE SPIRIT
### Love

The ethical side is, after all, the very core of Christ's work. Christ's mission to earth was to bring about an atonement for the sinner, and through His salvation to make the ungodly righteous. It is there He begins His work in the individual, namely in the area of justification by faith.

The instrument He equips with the gifts of the Spirit He desires to mold so that he also will bear the fruit of the Spirit. The molding of character is of greatest importance for the future full and proper manifestation of the gifts of the Spirit.

The ethical aspect of the work of the Spirit is presented in the Bible under the illustration of fruitbearing. Jesus expounds this truth in the parable of the vine and the branches. Paul, who gives us a detailed description of the Spirit, has also given a plain and clear presentation of the fruit of the Spirit. In his Epistle to the Galatians he writes:

"But the fruit of the Spirit is love, joy, peace, longsuffering, gentleness, goodness, faith, meekness, temperance" (Gal. 5:22, 23).

We live in a time when it is unpopular to speak of virtues, and when even Christians with some embarrassment hear themselves called "moralists." They do not like to be termed such. Virtue, however, is one of the values which never will decline in price nor be devalued. It has an eternal and constant value however much opinions may fluctuate. One may call darkness light, and one may say that black is white. Darkness is still darkness and black is black. Every human being knows and acknowledges this in the depth of his heart.

It is "the law of the Spirit of life" which makes us "free from the law of sin and death" (Rom. 8:2). Through a life in the fullness of the Spirit, a new law has entered our lives. Just as the works of the flesh dominated our lives before, so the fruit of the Spirit now begins to characterize them. Our life as Christians becomes the natural expression of the Spirit who dwells within us.

Love is first among the fruit of the Spirit. Love is an unsearchable phenomenon. It is like life in that it is totally unexplored in its essence and, next to life itself, still the greatest and mightiest factor in our existence. Where it is permitted to operate, it achieves incomprehensible results. Think of the sacrifices it has given, and the services it has rendered for the benefit of individuals as well as humanity at large. Love is surrounded by light and warmth. There it blossoms and only good fruit ripens in its presence.

Love actually radiates from God to all of humanity. He has supplied man with all necessities of life. If man had continued to walk in this love, all humanity today would have had everything needed for life and sustenance. It is man's lack of love which has caused all the want and sufferings he has passed through until this day.

When Christ in His discourse on the events of the last days says that "the love of many shall wax cold" (Matt. 24:12), He has reference, I am sure, not just to believers but to all people. There will come a time before the conclusion of the times of the Gentiles when lawlessness and sin shall increase to such an extent that the wonderful power of love which has meant so much throughout human history will lose its hold. Jesus uses fire as an illustration of love. Love shall wax cold, He says. He thus emphasizes the warmth which always accompanies true love. In a world full of sin it is cold, spiritually speaking, and in such a world love has had a tremendous task of spreading warmth and refreshing.

In our days plain family love is disappearing. The old-time love in lifelong marriages is also vanishing; love between parents and children, love between brothers and sisters which has been considered the purest and strongest of all love appears, in a frightening manner, to be cooling off.

Love which found an expression in one person's care for another in a wholesome community life and love between the nations is giving way to a heartless competition and armed aggression.

At such a time as ours, living Christianity with the gifts of the Spirit and the fruit of the Spirit can have a greater ministry than ever. Through the experience of the baptism in the Holy Spirit, God's love will be shed abroad in our hearts. It will be natural for us to love God above all else and our neighbor as ourselves. Our love for God will cause us unreservedly to give our lives back to Him. Our love for the brethren will tie us with unbreakable bands to the people of God. Our love for our fellowmen in general will cause us to give ourselves to the world for Christ. This love creates the fellowship with all God's people which can be termed the communion of saints.

* * *

## JOY IN GOD

Joy is an important factor in conjunction with the baptism in the Holy Spirit. The expressions of joy which have accompanied this experience have caused much discussion and to many it has actually become a stumbling stone. But joy is a consequence of the baptism in the Holy Spirit or, as the apostle Paul expresses it, a fruit of the Spirit. It cannot be separated from a real baptism in the Holy Spirit and the function of this fruit of the Spirit cannot be fully comprehended. Its influence reached from the gloom of everyday life to the hallowed ground stained by the martyrs' blood. It is this joy which bears up and lends charm to living Christianity even where it is faced with scorn and suffering unto death. It is the secret of the bright and happy Christianity which exists under most difficult circumstances; it caused the multitudes of martyrs to pass jubilantly through life and finally meet the end with joy. Without this explanation, their courage and shouts of victory would be incomprehensible. Their readiness to finish their days without a complaint, as the victims of the most atrocious injustice and in the deepest humiliation, betrays a powerful source of joy unknown to their environment. Theirs was the joy which is the fruit of the Spirit.

Joy, according to the apostle Paul, is the second-mentioned fruit of the Spirit. The angel announcing the birth of Jesus to the shepherds at Bethlehem proclaimed a message of joy: "I bring you good tidings of great joy, which shall be to all people" (Luke 2:10). Joy occupies a commanding place in the salvation Christ gives.

There is a natural need for joy in every human being, and the joy Jesus offers is for "all people." There is no condition which can hinder a person from partaking of this happiness. This is also the testimony everyone gives who has received the liberating power of living Christianity. They have become happy.

It is infinitely important that Christians become partakers of this joy in a full measure. This is where the baptism in the Holy Spirit fills a need which no other experience can satisfy. It is the Spirit who makes the divine realities living and real to the soul. He throws light upon the person and work of Christ and on all the treasures available to everyone who believes. He quickens the Word with all its promises and shows the joy of winning souls.

This fruit of the Spirit is necessary for every Christian. If he cannot get his desire for joy satisfied by God he will seek satisfaction in the pleasure of the world.

* * *

Much has been said about the evidence of the baptism in the Holy Spirit. One unquestionable sign that a person still lives in the fullness of the Spirit is that he possesses the joy of the Lord. This is a fruit of the Spirit which cannot be hidden. This joy cannot be mistaken for any other joy. Joking and jesting are always close at hand as substitutes for the joy in God, but they cannot truly take the place of salvation's joy. This joy bubbles up from the depth of the soul that is in a right relationship with God, and it puts on thanksgiving and praise to God like a garment. It often expresses itself in speaking in tongues when it experiences what the apostle Peter calls "joy unspeakable and full of glory."

A life in the divine love and joy presupposes peace with God through faith in our Lord Jesus Christ. Filled with this love and joy we have longsuffering, gentleness, goodness, faith, meekness, and temperance.

All of this belongs to the Spirit's ability to build character which is so necessary in order that the gifts of the Spirit may be used for the glory of God and the salvation of the world.

## SPIRITUAL MINISTRIES

Even as the Bible speaks of the gifts of the Spirit and the fruit of the Spirit, so it also mentions the ministries and miracles (operations, workings of power). The revival which will arise through the outpouring of the Spirit in the last days will proceed along the same lines as Christianity moved in apostolic days. The powerful outpouring of the Spirit which individuals at the early time experienced equipped them with everything they needed for the task. Preachers and leaders were taken directly from their secular work and went fully equipped because of what they had received through the Baptism in the Spirit.

They were, as the learned rabbis said, "uneducated, common men" (Acts 4:13 RSV), but the spiritual gifts and "workings of power," miracles, were manifested through them. When they were accused and threatened with imprisonment, the results of their work defended them. It is noted of Peter and John that when the council members saw "the man which was healed standing with them, they could say nothing against it" (Acts 4:14). Those who at any cost wanted to stop these men found themselves helpless! When the two fishermen from Galilee had left the hearing before the Sanhedrin, the chairman addressed the imposing array of spiritual leaders: "What shall we do to these men? for that indeed a notable miracle hath been done by them is manifest to all them that dwell in Jerusalem; and we cannot deny it" (Acts 4:16).

This is the kind of method the Holy Spirit used in apostolic days, and these same methods will characterize the revival of the last days. In these methods we see the secret of the rapid spread of Christianity during the first and second centuries. They were in no way dependent upon intellectual resources in their spiritual work. This will also be true in the coming revival. Only instruments who will submit themselves to the power and guidance of the Holy Spirit will be used. God uses tools who are willing, but He reserves the right to equip them as He pleases.

When the apostle Paul speaks of these work methods he says: "God hath set some in the church, first apostles, secondarily prophets, thirdly teachers, after that miracles, then gifts of healings, helps, governments, diversities of tongues" (I Cor. 12:28).

Because the simple apostolic method of working eventually was changed into several church organizations, these spiritual ministries were also changed into offices or, shall we say, professions. In many cases these ministries, without the spiritual equipment which was provided for them, have lost their spiritual content and functions.

When the apostle in conjunction with the distribution of ministries speaks of the church he has in mind the church in its universal sense. The ministry of the apostles did not belong to any one local church, neither did that of the prophets. In the Book of Acts we note that they traveled among the churches. This was true about Agabus who came from Judaea to Caesarea and there prophesied concerning the difficulties the apostle Paul would encounter during his continued travels. Those who had other ministries, such as teachers and evangelists, were also ambulating. In that manner all the local churches could partake of the various gifts which the Spirit in His divine wisdom distributed among these servants whom He led.

The office of an apostle, which was made an ecclesiastical principality, in reality was nothing like that. Theirs was the task of trailblazing and pioneering, but they were "uneducated, common men" without any claims of special dignity. The apostle Paul says that he was "less than the least"; and, no doubt, there were many among the apostles who, like Paul, devoted much time to physical labor.

If you would like to see a typical apostle of Jesus Christ, then imagine that one early morning somewhere around the year 50 A.D. you enter a tentmaker's shop in the Greek city of Corinth. The owner of the shop is a Jew by the name of Aquila. A short man, about 50 years of age, enters the shop and asks for a job. He shows his references. He learned the trade in Tarsus and has worked in a number of places since then. Although Aquila had just opened his business, he had a great deal of work lined up. The two men exchanged a few words about the work that should be done, and then it was decided that the man looking for employment could start right away.

This new employee was Paul, and soon you could see him working along with the rest of the workers. While the journeymen kept talking among themselves they eventually found out who Paul was.

On the sabbath he went with his employer to the synagogue and there he was asked to speak. Before long one of the largest and most influential churches of the first century blossomed around the simple little tentmaker. In that city, laying aside all his theological learning, he "determined not to know anything . . . save Jesus Christ, and him crucified" (I Cor. 2:2). During his spare time in this city he wrote the first of the epistles which has been preserved until our time, namely the first Epistle to the Thessalonians.

Between times he did missionary work amongst the fellows at the place of employment. They were the first to hear the profound thoughts about Christ and His atonement which we later see in Paul's writings.

It is not known whether Aquila and Priscilla were Christians when he started to work for them. They were Jews who had been ordered out of Rome, and Christianity had already reached the capital of the empire. If they were not Christians when Paul came to their shop, they might have been the first fruits of his apostolic ministry in Corinth.

When the highest and most influential of the spiritual ministries was so completely devoid of all ecclesiastical pomp and dignity, it is self-evident that the same is true about the other ministries which God has set in the church. Each one had specific gifts which were particularly developed, although they might have possessed other gifts of the Spirit.

The gift of prophecy had a prominent place in apostolic days — and this should be true at all times. In the great revival of the last days it will, no doubt, play an important role. In a different context we have spoken more in detail concerning this gift.

When it comes to the ministries of the teacher and the evangelist, we realize readily that they have an important place in a spiritual movement such as we are dealing with. Within the Pentecostal revival in various countries I have run into instances of one-sidedness which to a certain degree has become a liability of the movement. Younger preachers have pointed out that such conditions are a consequence of a lack of Bible teaching from the beginning. If the ministry of the teacher had been represented, the revival would have been much closer to the New Testament pattern than now is the case. We have examples of more than one outpouring of the Holy Spirit which, because of uncontrolled prophecies, went astray and was actually dissipated through lack of sound scriptural teaching.

The ministry of the evangelist is of basic importance. If outreach to unbelievers is repressed and is not permitted to be the main task of the Christian individual and of the local church, then stagnation and retrogression will be the natural consequences. That is why evangelists and teachers ambulated between the churches in apostolic days.

Something else in this context is, and will continue to be, of greatest importance, namely the guidance of the Spirit. Nowadays the churches generally call the evangelist and the teacher, but in apostolic times these ministers traveled under the direction of the Spirit. In that way they came at the right time to fields that were in need and ripe for the ministry they had.

All of this will be changed in the revival which is now at the door. Instead of churches and their leaders considering themselves as the directors of the Christian endeavor they will view their task in an altogether different way. The church's mission pertaining to those who have come to a living faith in Jesus is to care for them so that their spiritual life will endure and develop. It is this spiritual care which is the church's special responsibility toward the believers.

The church shall provide a platform for the evangelist and the teacher upon which they may minister. Therefore, the church must be open for this ministry when such persons, guided by the Holy Spirit, come to help the church.

The present pastoral system was nonexistent in apostolic days, and it will probably to a great extent be set aside in the outpouring of the Spirit in the last days. "Uneducated, common men" will take the positions of leadership in the revival movement which Christianity then will be. God will set in the church spiritual ministries in a far greater degree than we see now. These will be operating according to the guidance of the Spirit and this will be far more spiritually rewarding than to have officeholders who, by virtue of a majority vote, control Christian work.

As we have noted that the Lord chooses his servants without regard to education or special status, we are reminded of another side of His way of selecting which is no less remarkable, namely, the quality of the human material. One would think that He should pick people who had a good reputation and particularly people who had lived a life above reproach. But we find no such restrictions here either. He chooses and uses whoever comes to Him. He permits Judas to be in the circle of disciples and sent him out to preach and heal the sick. As long as he was honest and did not yield to criticism and betrayal he was allowed to participate.

Peter, who was self-confident, but a coward who denied His Lord when He most needed his faithfulness, was chosen for fantastic missions. One of His foremost ambassadors was chosen from the group of persecutors, a man who hunted down the followers of Jesus even in foreign cities.

In this way the Lord has made Himself independent of everything man considers great and a necessity for winning people for His cause. Whoever, in spite of his weaknesses, surrenders to Him, He will use in His service. This is the method He always used and, without a shadow of doubt, He will use it in the revival of the last days.

## A SPIRITUAL CHURCH LIFE
## DEMANDS SPIRITUAL QUALIFICATIONS

A ministry of a high spiritual standard must be built on people with spiritual qualifications. The church which was built in the apostolic era was founded and later carried by people dedicated to God and His cause. Their lives were no longer their own; their wishes and ambitions were consecrated once and for all on Christ's altar. They had personal experience of the words of Jesus: "Whosoever will lose his life for my sake shall find it" (Matt. 16:25). Christ was their life, and His cause alone occupied and dominated their longings and desires.

They were gripped by one mission alone, namely to rescue their neighbors from a life in sin and bring them to happiness and victory in fellowship with God.

This was true in the highest degree about the leaders of the Christian movement. If we examine the people whose history is most complete, we find that they were 100 percent surrendered to Christ and His cause. There were halfhearted people, to be sure, both amongst the preachers and the lay-leaders, but these were not the ones who built the Christian church nor molded it. It was those totally committed leaders who, although they were not perfect in themselves but just plain, weak human beings, formed the character of the church of the apostolic era.

There are two extremes which threaten all movements of this kind. Most of the revival movements during the course of history have become victims of one of these. The one temptation is to organize the movement and in this way take the leadership. The other temptation is to gather the work of God around a person and make him the sole leader. Whoever assumes the leadership of such a movement from the beginning will choose the course, and from then on the movement will follow that direction.

If the organizational path is followed, then usually the most prominent man becomes the leader of the denomination; thus he receives a privileged position which, of course, can give opportunity for satisfaction of personal demands and desires.

If following the course of personal leadership, the movement gives the leader the opportunity to build up a work around himself, personal freedom and authority become boundless. In some instances this kind of personal initiative may be justified. When the local church does not fulfill her calling, but leaves areas of ministry untouched which should be her concern, then it is only proper that private initiative step in.

The Pentecostal movement in Sweden has chosen the autonomous church as the vehicle for God's work.

We have not had any denominational organization we could lean on. The local churches, as they were established, tried to do what they could, but it could never be enough for the very extensive ministry which has been carried on. And in the early days before any churches were established, even then an extensive ministry was carried on, and it depended almost entirely upon personal contributions and sacrifices.

In order to build up a work of this kind, it is apparent that there must be people who are willing to give up their personal interests. Gripped by Christ and His cause, they must be willing to make any sacrifice. Personal, as well as financial advantages, must not influence their decision.

The way of the local church principle, however glorious it may be, makes great demands upon those who embrace it. Everything is sacrificed for this common cause. In the early church, people had all things in common. On this road the pastor must lead the way. He sacrifices his time, his strength, his talents, his initiative, his ideas — everything must be on the altar.

He must place his most intimate and dearest interest on the altar of God and of the church. His family must come second; although they may not need to suffer want, they still have to make sacrifices for the common good. Only with a living faith in God is the pastor able to assume the responsibility of permitting children of his own, as well as from other families, to suffer the consequences of the self-denials such families have submitted themselves to. Such were the demands upon the leadership of the early Christian church. If one desires to build a spiritual ministry of the same kind as they, one must be willing to pay the same price.

Those who built the apostolic church never looked upon the work as their own. I am sure an expression such as "my church" was never heard. No, the church was looked upon as a work of God for which Christ was the Head. Thus the direction of the church came from higher authority. The Holy Spirit was a reality in their lives and ministry. He led them both in decisions which had to be made as well as in the planning and execution of the work. They were instruments in God's hand and nothing else. Their service was a work of faith which engendered love, wisdom, and power for the superhuman task they had been assigned.

All of this brought them in close contact with the eternal world. The values of that world were concrete realities to them. Surrounded by its light they gave their lives with joy for their Lord and Master. This attitude created the heavenly and divine atmosphere which we meet in the New Testament church life. It is a fantastic experience, that even today in a time like ours, we can sense the same divine Presence in the Christian church.

The church was not primarily a work organ, with a board and a chairman like any human organization, but it was a divine organism whose mission was to care for the jewels which Christ had bought with His own blood. This was the task the apostle Paul referred to in his touching farewell to the elders of the then modern commercial city of Ephesus; these elders were shepherds chosen by the Holy Spirit. Paul himself, the genuine lay preacher, had a need of reminding them of his unselfish example: "Yea, ye yourselves know, that these hands have ministered unto my necessities, and to them that were with me, I have shewed you all things, how that so labouring ye ought to support the weak" (Acts 20:34, 35).

It was this unselfishness, this unwearied ministry without thought of personal gain and sacrifices, which created the kind of invincible Christianity and church life they had in apostolic times.

This unselfishness is the basic element in Christianity. It was this which compelled Jesus during His sacrificial ministry throughout life and finally caused Him to give Himself to the death of the cross. It was this same sacrificial spirit which compelled John the Baptist in his unselfish life and martyr's death. It was this unselfish contribution the apostles made when they gave their lives to spread Christ's teaching, and in the process all of them, possibly with the exception of John, suffered a martyr's death.

This is the way those have trodden who have been instruments who have shaken peoples, nations, and churches until a riverbed was prepared for the river of life; a riverbed which again and again has been obstructed or dammed up by ecclesiastical debris or by a society hostile to God.

There are those who believe that in our modern day there

is an easier way to victory for the Christian church, but he who would reach the goal of the apostolic day must walk the narrow way of the apostolic times.

# VI

# The De-Christianization
# Of Our Society

The church of today has given more attention to herself and her own problems than to the world she was commissioned to save for her Lord and Savior.

Her task, according to Christ's program, has been to be salt in a world which is putrefying. She was meant to be the light of the world. But this light has been sealed off too much by an introverted self-centeredness.

The motivation for this isolation has been that the church should keep herself unpolluted by the world. Many have been busy about the unification of Christians, something which ought to be self-evident to anyone who knows what the unity of the Spirit is. They have managed to amalgamate churches and to increase the number of organizations, but the influence of the church in the world has been constantly diminishing.

During the last decades one country after another has been closed to the Gospel. In the so-called Christian countries the Christian influence has been forced to retreat from public life more and more.

While the anti-Christian propaganda has been extremely active and has made our society as a whole the object of its efforts, the Christian church has carried on its ministry primarily inside her churches and prayer chapels. The non-Christians have been engaged in the social concerns, while the Christians have shied away from them.

In a remarkable way the church has been able to ignore the fact that the development of our society to a great extent depends on its leadership. Turning away from this reality the church has failed to exert its influence in this area.

During the last few decades in Sweden, in America, and in most countries of our western culture, there are particularly three thought patterns which have influenced our society, namely, Marxism, Freudianism, and relativism. Each one of these in its own way has made infractions on Christian morality, which by and large had dominated in the countries of our western culture.

Since Marxism has made such inroads among the workers in our modern industrial society, the result has been an enormously powerful anti-Christian influence. From the working man's viewpoint this political philosophy has appealed to his purely material interests. Many of the demands of the workers have been just. When the leaders of the labor movement, who have presented these demands, have made known their sympathies with Marxism, it has been quite easy to accept the atheistic elements with the materialistic ones of this philosophy.

Especially in the countries where the labor movement has adhered to Marxism, its materialism and atheism have leavened the thinking of the masses.

In this context the church has a tremendous responsibility. Sweden is a typical example. There the labor movement began right on the heels of a Christian revival. The first strike took place among the workers at the sawmills near Sundavall (a city in northern Sweden), because the employers took steps against the workers. In the name of justice this had to be corrected. This concerted action in the interest of the laborers was spearheaded by the believing workers.

Neither the church nor the Christians outside the church realized the opportunity to plead the cause of the laborers who were fighting a tough battle. But there were others who were interested in the labor movement – others who had been under the influence of the Marxist labor movement in Germany. When they offered their leadership, the future of the Swedish labor movement was sealed and delivered to a Marxist ideology. What this has meant for Christian development in Sweden is known to all who are acquainted with the conditions in this Nordic land.

Similar situations, no doubt, have existed in other countries also where the labor movement now is under Marxist leadership.

It is also a known fact what Sigmund Freud's partly misinterpreted psychoanalysis has meant to the world. The overemphasis on sexuality, which has become a consequence of his teachings, is now beginning to bear fruit in many countries, not least in Sweden.

An examination undertaken by this writer of the official records of the Swedish Riksdag proved that the Freudian teaching had influenced our legislation to a high degree.

Before 1930, that was before Freud propounded his theses, several motions were brought before the Riksdag to soften the marriage and other related laws, but such motions generally speaking failed to carry for lack of support. But after Freud's views had been disseminated, changes of laws have taken place as fast as if done on an assembly line. Sex education has been introduced to our elementary schools and high schools, and what is taught is certainly absolutely contrary to Christian morality. At the same time, prayer and Christian instruction have been banned from the schools. In fact, authorities have even forbidden table prayers in the dining rooms provided by the social services for the little children.

With sex education, measures have followed among children and young people which only a few years ago would have seemed unbelievable. Vending machines making prophylactics available right on the school grounds and the assertion that young people have every right to sexual intercourse before marriage have broken down all barriers. Our country has become known all over the world as the champion of loose morality.

It must be added, however, that the Swedish people in general are not on such a low level of morality. It is hardly likely that the majority of the labor party are in sympathy with this immorality, even though they belong to the ruling party which to a great extent is responsible for more deterioration in our country.

Relativism has its basis in the so-called Uppsala philosophy, which is promulgated by some who hold that there are no absolute norms. The attack has been directed not only against the Christian ethic but also against the eternal truths or verities mentioned by Plato and the Greeks: the true, the good, and the beautiful.

According to relativism there is no absolute truth, nothing is absolutely good, and nothing is absolutely beautiful. What is true to one is not true to another; what is good to one is not good to another; and what is beautiful to one is not beautiful to another. There are no fixed norms. Everything is in a flux, even the living habits of children and young people.

One is amazed at the very idea that children and young people don't need any fixed norms. One cannot imagine that they would adhere to this principle in other areas of our dealings between people.

In Sweden we have recently introduced right-hand traffic. Just think what it would look like if we had applied the principle of relativism to this change. How would it work out, if we departed from certain set norms which now govern traffic and instead each one was permitted to drive according to his own liking?

But the authorities which otherwise accept relativism are smart enough not to endorse such an experiment. How frightening then that they dare support absence of standards and traffic rules on the great highway of life. No wonder our young people become victims of all kinds of catastrophies.

The absence of such norms and guidelines has resulted in youth problems of alcoholism, drug abuse, disobedience to parents and insubordination to teachers.

The so-called educated young people at our universities are, unfortunately, the leaders in disregard and disrespect of norms, laws and ordinances. This is a catastrophe in a modern society, where relativism has been made the traffic ordinance for the highway of life.

It is in this general area of concern that Christians by their leadership in our society should have been a force to hinder the moral deterioration and the deep spiritual darkness which now prevail.

What we now experience of violence, terror, and horror is nothing but the fruit of what has been sown, namely egotism, materialism, and hatred. Why be surprised over what we reap, when we consider what has been sown? It would be more strange if we did not, for then the world and its laws would indeed be turned upside down. How would we then know the laws that govern human intercourse here on earth? As it is, the law of sowing and reaping is maintained, in spite of the infractions governments and legislatures have made on many natural rules of life.

Even the busy sowers themselves can see how their sowing of egotism and hatred is beginning to ripen into "grapes of wrath," as one American author has well put it. These "grapes" are now ripening toward the day when everyone shall receive the things done in his body. Believe me, this applies to politics and politicians as well.

Jesus speaks of two phenomena which shall follow each other very closely in the closing days of time, namely lawlessness and lovelessness. "Due to exorbitant lawlessness, the love of many shall be chilled" (Matt. 24:12 Berk. ver.).

These words have generally been applied to the Christian church as though the Bible and God's care did not include the whole world. But the laws and promises of the Bible apply to all men.

The Bible has much to say about loving our neighbor. Upon this kind of love human society was meant to be built.

Consider in this context the importance of family love. Independent of all social institutions, this peculiar force, unexplored by science, has caused people to care for and to work for the good of one another. Think of the joy and happiness produced by this unselfish love. It would be impossible to describe the harvests of good fruits it has brought about.

At the same time, any society which has rid itself of the "love, which is the perfect bond of union" (Col. 3:14 Berk. ver.) has experienced a deep-freezing of all higher values. Theirs has been the sterility of desert lands, and theirs the fruit of thorns and thistles.

Characteristic of our day is lawlessness. Vanishing parental authority, and contempt of the laws of the land and of all true values describe our times. License and immorality are a part of the contemporary scene. Doctors, police, and authorities are viewed as the enemies of our society and are exposed to contempt and sabotage, and the end is not in sight.

It is lamentable and threatening to observe these tendencies among our children and young people, but it is even more deplorable that many elderly people defend this lawlessness. And worse yet is the fact that this license is used for political ends. There are politicians who will not hesitate to endorse this kind of spirit in order to gain a few votes at an election — a gruesome practice, indeed!

Once hatred and violence have at their disposal as formidable instruments of destruction as is now the case we are not far from a world catastrophe. In the violent clashes we now have between races, classes and political ideologies, a spark may be produced which will start a world conflagration.

If the world ever needed a new spirit in its politics it certainly does today.

Who but the Christians, gripped by their love for their neighbor, can bring about such a spirit!

Apart from total destruction of everything which western culture has built up, there is only one alternative, namely a spiritual revival which will convey divine love to the Christian church as well as to our modern society in general.

Jesus was once asked some questions concerning our love for our neighbor. And He answered by telling the parable of the Good Samaritan. He portrays humanity's need, and shows how one person must care for the other.

Many Christians confine their concern to the Christian brethren — if they go that far. In Christ's parable I assume that these are likened to the priest and the Levite, who were so taken up with their religious duties in Jerusalem that they had neither time nor opportunity to pay any attention to the stricken fellow traveler along their pathway.

This is a striking picture of today's Christianity. Christian love of today does not extend itself as far as to the society which, spiritually speaking, has fallen in the hands of thieves, and which is now bleeding to death at the church doors. Just as Jesus predicted, "the love of many" has been chilled. The care for the wounded is left to the Samaritan with whom one has no religious fellowship.

Christians assume a great deal of the responsibility for the hordes of vandals which now are trying to take over our modern society. Those who could have initiated a policy of love have often refused to give their support to the upbuilding of our society.

Is it possible that Christians even in days to come will continue to be indifferent and cold before the Christian commandment of love?

What modern society really cries for is a policy built on love for the neighbor.

However materialistic the policy of a country may be, it is always inspired by a spirit, a keynote, a disposition. It is this spirit which determines the direction and aims of a political movement. It creates its very atmosphere and its power of action. If a spirit of hatred is in control, then the policy will be dominated by egotism, jealousy, and force. If on the other hand, love is the guiding star, then the motto will be: "All things whatsoever ye would that men should do to you, do ye even so to them."

## DISAPPOINTED YOUNG PEOPLE

It is not difficult to understand that young people in our

days are resorting to narcotics and alcohol with the behavioral pattern which follows. They have nothing to live for. They have hardly any future here on earth, and many do not believe in a future life.

The future they might envision would be to reach some of the very peaks of the society they fight for. But even those in highest leadership have very insecure positions. We need only mention names like Stalin, Molotov, Khrushchev.

If these young people are thinking of the status of the common laborer in the Neo-Marxist society this is not a very attractive goal. Compared with workers in other countries they are far worse off then others. They do not have better economic conditions, and above all they have no freedom. They do not have the right to speak up and voice their opinion, nor can they hold a personal faith and propagate it as the workers in democratic countries may. Their political and cultural freedom is regulated by military force as so recently has happened in Czechoslovakia. This is the future that young people of our modern society may look forward to.

Most young people can now get an education and aim at a white-collar job. But the trouble is that all young people have this goal in mind. There will be such an over-supply of this kind of worker that only a very few of the applicants will find any employment openings. This may lead to a change in income for office personnel so that this type of employee may be considered a low income group. Then the shrinking supply of laborers may cause their wages to rise — which would be a fair adjustment.

For a long time they have carried on the heaviest work for the lowest wage.

This is the kind of future our contemporary youth may have to look forward to. In days gone by they could have planned to start some private enterprise, but this will hardly be possible in days ahead in socialistic countries.

There was a time when young people could save funds toward starting their own business. This is hardly possible in countries which are under a socialist system. No one can save anything, for the taxes eat up the savings of the young people and leave them with empty hands when they are about to start out in life.

Society has assumed the responsibility for their upbringing. From the day they are born they are living on government subsidies, spend their days in special child-care centers, have free schooling with food and books gratis. They enjoy a free university education, receive special government scholarships, and can arrange for advantageous loans. All these items are considered great privileges; a country that offers them to their people is called a welfare state.

But all of this, and more, the parents are paying for through taxes. And as soon as the young people themselves begin to earn an income they have to start to pay for what they thought they had received free of charge from the state.

The system works this way: instead of letting people take care of their own savings and use them at their own discretion, they have to turn them over to the state in the form of taxes and then the state pays back their own funds in the form of special government benefits.

This is really one way of saying that the individual citizen cannot be considered of age, and therefore the state has to serve as a legal guardian of the individual.

Nowadays some forward boys and girls make themselves the spokesmen of youth and inspire them to follow in demonstrations and political expressions of liberty. These front figures are the standard-bearers of the young, they have good prospects of having a place in the sun in the Marxist society. They will constitute the upper class in the kind of state they are fighting for. Those who follow them will be the pariahs of the new society or the tax-paying serfs of the welfare state. It will continue to be a class society though structured somewhat differently. That is all.

In reality this is actually a return to slavery, but in a slightly changed form. The difference is that now the state owns the means of production, which corresponds to the plantations of the slave owners of old.

It is this kind of slavery which will constitute the future of our young people. Could it be that though they may not see this, they have a strange unconscious presentiment of it and therefore in their disillusionment turn to narcotics, alcohol, and immorality?

Young people in the olden days as a rule dreamed of a happy home. Marriage loomed ahead as a secluded paradise where one would live together with one's great love.

There one would enjoy the happiness of matrimonial cohabitation which before had been out of bounds. It was generally held in those days that one ought not to engage in sexual relationships before one had officially assumed the responsibility for any and all consequences. One had to feel responsible for children who might be the result of such cohabitation – responsible before both children and authorities.

This matrimonial happiness consisted in part in the fact that after the wedding one was fully entitled to this kind of cohabitation. This had not been tried before and within bounds of marriage seemed so attractive. Young people looked forward to it and to living together with the one they loved.

By and large, young people today cannot look forward to such a happiness. If they are particularly fond of someone, they have often left absolutely nothing of marital cohabitation untried. The fences around the holy area of sexual relations have long ago been broken down. What they on their honeymoon should have experienced as something new and as an exciting and beautiful introduction to married life has long ago been consumed as forbidden fruit on forbidden ground.

Many young people are tired of the world they have entered – a world without goal, interest and meaning. They try to escape from its gloomy reality by means of intoxication, which for a few moments makes life a little bit happier. This is why alcohol and narcotics have such an attraction.

This is the real background to young people's attraction to intoxicating drinks and narcotics. Unsatisfied souls experience a kind of release and a lift as they take these intoxicants, and this is the explanation of the drug and alcohol abuses raging without control among our young people.

It is not hard to understand that young people of today are longing for something to take the place of the real life values which the youth of past generations were confronted with and assimilated. Past generations of young people could center their interest around so many material, spiritual and idealistic values which just do not exist anymore.

There are many reasons, other than religious, for limiting sexual relations to married life. For their own good every individual and every state ought to adopt this as a rule of life.

One need not be a Christian in order to appreciate good, moral living, happy family relations, and a sober and well-ordered community life. Without this status no human being can feel satisfied with his existence. A living faith in God is an additional, tremendous strength — not least for a young person. It is this which like nothing else gives content and meaning to life.

In times past a young person's mind was filled with material, idealistic, and spiritual aspirations, but today these have to retreat before the one thing which dominates the present — a casual drive, sexuality. This is what dominates literature, film, theater, press, radio and TV; it is the all-absorbing interest.

Since this sex mania came and conquered, and even our schools have been turned into hotbeds of this kind of supersexuality, it would be no surprise if our young people should become fed up with this unnatural immorality. They have had enough of this drive of freedom to do anything they please, and they do not know what to do. That is why it is so natural for them to turn to narcotics and alcohol.

In this way disappointed young people are produced in assembly-line fashion.

# VII

# The Gospel - The Power Of God

## THE LAW OF THE SWINGING PENDULUM

There are some natural laws which appear to be very simple, but in reality they are as mysterious as the universe in its entirety. One of these is the law of the swinging pendulum. Its principle touches almost the secret of the concept of perpetual motion, which is defined as "an hypothetical machine perpetually supplying its own motive forces independent of any action from without" (Webster).

The secret of the pendulum is that it moves by its own weight. It is the weight of the pendulum which gets it into motion, and when it has moved as far as the pendulum rod permits, it will return by its own weight.

One can see some evidence of this law almost everywhere. Not a creature, not anything is totally void of this law. Anyone or anything which swings too far in one direction will sooner or later swing back to the opposite extreme. If an exaggeration occurs in one direction, it is certain to be repeated in the opposite one also.

All of creation and the tremendous mobility which characterizes the same are based on balance. The universe, the various worlds which travel at the speed of light between and past each other, must maintain their mobility within designated bounds. Should any stellar body leave its orbit and not stay in its designated course, it would probably result in a universal catastrophe which man always has feared would come — the end of the world..

If we turn to history we will find the same principle there.

The world has throughout the ages been pendulating from one extreme to the other. The great oscillations of the pendulum of the world are the cultures which like mighty waves have carried humanity from primitivism, ignorance and poverty to refinement, intellectualism, and financial affluence.

But history also demonstrates that when these cultures reach their acme, the pendulum will return. The pendulum slows down in its upward swing, it stops eventually, a millionth of a second it remains immobile, then there is a slight quiver, and weighted by its own nature it begins the downward swing.

In our days, a time which has dubbed itself the knight of intellectualism, every school child knows that this has been the tale of all cultures. Do we have any reason to believe that our culture will not share the same fate as all previous ones?

In politics we find the same conditions. There the pendulum begins its swing upward from social injustices, the wealth owned by a few individuals, and the ruling power of the society in the hands of the rich elite. Injustices have gone too far. The selfishness of the ruling clique and their suppressing of the rights of others give impetus to dissatisfaction among more and more citizens until the political power is distributed and placed in the hands of the people. A democratic breakthrough comes with an equitable sharing of the good of society.

The new ruling class, however, will have the same experience as their predecessors. Once they have gained the power, they think only of their own party, their own sympathizers, and their own political position. True, a different segment of society, and perhaps a larger representation, has control of the good of society, but it continues to be a society of classes. The difference is only that another segment is in power, just as egoistic and class-conscious as the old leadership ever was.

This is an indication that the pendulum is about to reach its acme. A democratic rule is also subject to the law of the swinging pendulum. Many believe that a political trend can continue to be more and more radical, but this is not the case. In ancient Rome the pendulum swung from a republic to a triumvirate to an empire. Control and balance in nature and in existence will never cease. You can just as well try to make a pendulum continue to swing ever upward or try to keep it at its acme as to ignore the equilibrium and balance present in all normal situations in our existence.

The spiritual life in the world is subject to the same laws. This life is never stagnant, but it is continually moving in rising or falling waves. The early church began a rising curve which maintained its strength a long time until the spiritual power was drained and substituted by organizations, doctrines and ceremonies. The paralyzing pressure of the Catholic church threatened to annihilate the simple, living movement which began with the carpenter from Nazareth and the fishermen from the sea of Tiberias.

The law of the swinging pendulum, however, applied also in this context. With Christendom at a bottom position during medieval times, there were reformers, torchbearers, who could bring light to the multitudes groping in ecclesiastical darkness until times of spiritual revival and renewal would come. From the 1300's this spiritual springtime increased and spread through many movements by many different names. The reform and revival movements of the 1500's and 1600's grew into the great awakenings of the 19th and 20th centuries.

An intellectualism which has been carried too far, criticism of the supernatural element in Christianity and an altogether too "blue-eyed" faith in organization and collectivism have in no small degree depleted Christianity of its spiritual power. A fighting atheism intending to de-Christianize schools and universities, has made inroads among the youth of our day, and succeeded in removing large multitudes of young people from Christian influence. The profanation of marriage, the breakdown of family life, and a godless and immoral life of entertainment have made a large section of our contemporary fellowmen unreceptive toward the Christian message.

There are, however, signs indicating that we have reached the very bottom position. Man has been over-stuffed with materialism and atheism. Looseness among young people has gone so far that emancipated young people themselves begin to realize the unnatural and dangerous in their situation. The leaders who believed and proclaimed that norms are a kind of slavery which we can get along without now have experienced just a little too much of the behavior of these unprincipled youths.

Teachers, jurists, and authorities begin to understand that lawlessness will not create any ideal society. The spiritual leaders also realize that the responsibility of Christianity is not just limited to the church, but it must be extended to the world by which she is surrounded. But if the contemporary situation has reached a spiritual bottom position, is there any hope for better days ahead? Will the pendulum begin the upward swing again? I believe we can discover a gleam of light in the spiritual emergency; that gleam of light is a new outpouring of the Holy Spirit.


## THE GOSPEL – THE POWER OF GOD

When Christianity is recommended as the cure of the ills of our time, one obviously wants to show some concrete examples of how the Gospel has demonstrated its exceptional power.

Neither would it be right in this kind of a setting to bypass the prominent place philanthropy occupies in the teaching and practice of Christ and His apostles – and also in the modern Pentecostal movement.

We are therefore justified in including an account of our labors among the outcasts of society, even if it will have to be brief for the sake of space.

Ever since I began my ministry in Stockholm as the pastor of the Filadelfia Church, the poor and the victims of alcohol had a prominent place in my work schedule. It all started with daily visits by these unfortunates whom I personally received. I distributed lodging and food tickets as long as the solicited funds would last. Later on, the work was expanded to include off-street shelters, a couple of ships remodeled for sleeping quarters, and large-scale feedings of the needy during the depression years in the 30's.

It happened on a Sunday morning, I was still preparing for the sermon I was to preach in about an hour. Then someone rang my doorbell, and when I opened I found a man asking for some assistance. He was poorly dressed, holes in his shoes, and a worn overcoat. He had turned up the collar and tied a string around it to keep it up. The temperature was 5-10 degrees below zero, and he looked as though he were frozen stiff. He told me that he had walked all night, because he had no place to sleep, and then he asked for some money to buy a cup of coffee. I gave him enough to buy what he had requested. He thanked me and was gone.

There I stood in my warm bachelor's quarters, at that time a modern and attractive one-bedroom apartment. I was shaken. Soon I would be facing the well-dressed and well-cared-for congregation which now was gathering for their morning worship. I was to preach His Gospel who said: "I was hungered, and ye gave me meat. . . . I was a stranger, and ye took me in," but what was I doing for these children of misfortune?

That Sunday morning I spoke to the congregation with deep feeling because of the personal encounter I had had that very day with the acute social needs of man. I appealed to the assembly to help me do something for the people who existed in the shadows of life, and I was fully determined to do something for these out and outers, regardless of the response. My points were well-received, and this led to the beginning of this type of ministry.

Poverty and material distress were much greater in Swedish society at that time than they are today. The entire structure of our society has changed much during the last fifty years.

The needs, however, are just as great today, if not greater, with this difference only, that they are found in other areas. And our rescue efforts have been adapted to the changing situation. Today the slaves of evil habits, their families, criminality and its victims are the focal point of need. To help them we established a foundation a few years ago.

In conjunction with my seventieth birthday, friends of mine initiated a fund drive which brought in about 200,000 Swedish kronor (approximately $40,000), and this became the starting capital for the "Lewi Pethrus' Foundation for Philanthropic Ministry." This foundation is an independent institution which is primarily tied to the Pentecostal movement which has given it the strongest support.

The ministry of this foundation during the last years under the energetic and prudent leadership of Erik Edin has had a phenomenal growth.

Our policy is to try to help the victims of alcohol and narcotics to start a new life on a Christian basis. Even though the intentions and decisions of those people be ever so upright, they need practical help, to begin with, in the form of a rehabilitation program. As far as we are concerned, this has opened the door to a spiritual ministry and rebuilding of lives. By the grace of God and through the assistance of our friends, we have been able to extend such help to our clients.

The people we help are generally destitute. They need help for their temporal needs in every detail. Their economy must be straightened out, and their family problems solved. The wives and children are especially worthy of consideration in this type of rescue ministry.

We believe that a thoroughgoing experience of salvation through Jesus Christ is the best cure for all evil habits. It has also been proven that just such an experience has delivered those who were firmly chained by alcoholism, narcotics, and criminality.

The Pentecostal movement is making exceptional contributions in the worldwide ministry among alcoholics and narcotics addicts. The outstanding work among the addicts in the United States which David Wilkerson, founder of Teen Challenge, described in the book, *The Cross and the Switchblade,* is known all over the world. Hand in hand with the message of Pentecost a great rescue ministry is carried on around the earth. Fantastic miracles of deliverance from these chains of habits and their terrible consequences take place. Lasting results of the Teen Challenge ministry can be read in the other books by David Wilkerson as well as in those by Nicky Cruz, Sonny Arguinzoni, Bob Bartlett, Herbert Walker, and Floyd Miles.

What we are doing in Stockholm in this mission field is also done by local churches throughout Sweden but on a smaller scale.

As proof of the wonderful power of the Gospel in this area I consider it in order to present a few examples of what God is able to do.

At a ministers' conference in the city of Uppsala, Sweden in 1955 I saw Erik Edin for the first time. He had recently been converted and gave his personal testimony. He stressed the unhappy plight of the alcoholics and of their families and seemed to feel out the preachers if anything more could be done to rescue the slaves of this habit. I felt very sympathetic toward him, and thought of a possibility of using him in a ministry to alcoholics.

At that time I was the pastor of the Filadelfia Church in Stockholm. I extended an invitation to him to come to us for a service. After that he was called to head up a ministry to victims of alcoholism. In 1960 he was asked to direct the Lewi Pethrus' Foundation for Philanthropic Ministry; he accepted and has been very successful in his work.

A unique feature of this foundation is that all department heads of the organization are former alcoholics or former narcotics addicts. I have found that they are especially well-qualified for such a position. They know the difficulties and battles of the clients, and they know better than anyone else what can help them. To see their love for their former brothers in misery is a gripping experience.

Here follow the testimonies of some of the men who now are employed by the foundation in this rescue mission work. They are men who are "as a firebrand plucked out of the fire."

First, the director of the foundation, Erik Edin:

"I was a captive of most habits and vices which in a catastrophic way pull down human beings. My own family and the authorities considered me a hopeless case — impossible to rehabilitate to a normal life. I was an incurable alcoholic. I simply could not live without alcohol. My inner being cried for a glass of liquor. There was a craving for satisfaction but in a form which had become a curse to me. The liquor thirst was like hellfire within me. On top of this I had committed some criminal acts. In several ways I had broken the laws of Sweden. For years I had been in and out of different hospitals and institutions.

"Such was my condition and situation the night I experienced a transformation. I was strolling up and down the streets of Uppsala, a human being in ruins, a social catastrophe case, burnt out in body and soul, fully conscious that I had only three alternatives: suicide, mental institution, prison.

"In this desperate situation I went to the Filadelfia Church of that city, a last way out, before I intended to take the consequences of my sinful life, and bring to an end my miserable life.

"At that time in the evening I could expect that the service would be just about over, so I felt free to enter the church as dirty and shabbily dressed as I was. It seemed impossible for me in my physical humiliation to actually sit down in a church pew amongst worshiping people.

"As I came into the sanctuary the service was still in progress; people were listening to the string band which was singing and playing the concluding numbers.

"I stood inside the swinging doors and had not been there many seconds before I was gripped by the Spirit prevailing in the service. It was the same loving and good Spirit I had met during my childhood and adolescence. Standing there I saw before my inner eyes my whole life as in review; there were all my miserable failures in life, and anew I felt the depth of my despair which I so often had suffered because of my sin.

"The periods I had spent in prisons and institutions came vividly before me. In a horribly realistic way I experienced the grip sin had on me. It was an iron grip which made me conscious in my very heart of hearts that I was a slave under desires whose iron chains I simply could not break with any human help.

"I realized that my case was so utterly hopeless that if I had asked my own father for help he would have been unable to do anything for me. It was useless to spend any effort on me.

"In whatever direction I turned it was as though I only heard a terrible No! No! No!

"Standing there inside the church doors with these thoughts of hopelessness and despair, all of a sudden I felt the atonement of Jesus Christ become very real to me. With my inner vision I saw Him walking the road to Calvary with heavy steps. Afterward I realized that it was the instruction I had received as a child in Sunday school and what I had heard when as a young lad I attended church with my mother which now came back to me. It was deep down there in my dark and sinful heart. Now it was quickened by the Holy Spirit. This experience connected my thoughts with something new and something unexpected in my situation. Suddenly I realized that Christ's atonement was for me. The drama on Calvary's hill was for my salvation. My thoughts reached for something so unbelievable to me: there is forgiveness, salvation and restoration.

"Thousands of times I have tried to describe what actually happened in that moment, but I have never been able to do it — and cannot do it now either. Words cannot express this glorious experience of seeing a spark of hope in the midst of the deepest depth of despair.

"Then it happened. Slowly and with hesitant steps I

walked down the aisle. As I came to the mourner's bench I dropped to my knees. I began to weep, and my lips stuttered a prayer — it was the painful and sincere prayer for mercy and forgiveness by a prodigal son. 'If it is true that You loved me so much that You died for me, then I want to live for You or die.'

"Just how long I remained in prayer and weepingly poured out my heart before the Lord, I don't know. But when I arose, something remarkable had happened to me. I was a different person. A transformation had taken place in my inner man.

"My clothes were just as shabby, my hair just as long and ungroomed, I was just as dirty, all my crimes and offenses against individuals and our society were still there, and my home about 250 miles away was just as poor. My wife and children were in the same poverty as before.

"BUT I WAS SAVED, TRANSFORMED, AND RESCUED!"

The next remarkable testimony which I would like to share is by a prominent businessman, a civil engineer, Sten Arnell, who was completely ruined by alcohol, but who was saved through faith in Jesus. Now he heads up the foundation's industries for the rehabilitation of alcoholics and drug addicts.

He says:

"Since ten years ago I am a fully rehabilitated former alcoholic, and I have spent much time studying alcoholism, and especially tried to penetrate my own behavior pattern and my evaluation during all the years before I became an alcoholic. Five years of alcoholism were a hell on earth. But I also know of many years as a total abstainer and as an harmonious man.

"When the question is raised — and it often is — why I used alcohol and why I became an alcoholic, I answer clearly and with conviction that I at that time lived without God, and I believed that I was self-sufficient, that success in business and the social life which accompanies it would lead to happiness for me and my family.

"But the success I sought and gained in this way could not take away an ever-increasing restlessness in my inner man, a restlessness I tried to quiet first with moderate, then increased liquor consumption and finally by abuse of alcohol. When every morning I was compelled by my own body to take a few drinks before I could meet the daily tasks, then I began to realize what alcoholism really is.

"My misery continued for yet some years, my wife sued for and got her divorce, and I had to leave our children with her. Doctors, rest homes, hospitals could not help me. My friends began to withdraw from me. I was no longer the effective and successful industrial leader. In 1958 I lost my elegant home in one of the suburbs of Stockholm and moved into a miserable little rented room near the city. Earlier I had made a serious attempt to take my own life, but now I didn't even have strength enough to do that. I lay there completely exhausted with the anguish of despair at the thought of another day. Forsaken and forgotten, I was unable to take care of myself.

"Just imagine if I at that time and even earlier had known and realized that my dissatisfaction, my restlessness and finally my going downhill depended on the fact that I turned my back to God, and that I thought the message about Jesus was only for a little group of good, but mediocre and ineffective people. Today I know better.

"Unfortunately there is a widely accepted misunderstanding concerning the hundreds of thousands in our little country alone who every year become victims of alcoholism and that is that they come from some special social sector of society, and that they from childhood and adolescence lived under such conditions where they were not properly trained by parents and schools, and that they already in their childhood home became social misfits and therefore became predestined to a life of alcoholism. At the same time one is often inclined to ascribe to the alcoholic a low I.Q. and a lack of intellectual interests.

"It is true that alcoholics from such a milieu and with such characteristics make up a large segment which becomes noticeable in official statistics from police and temperance boards. Even temperance boards, however, know that at one time the majority of their clients were in such social circumstances that they did not need any assistance from their board.

"The problem of alcoholism in Sweden is, indeed, great, and if the statistics of the temperance boards could be related to realities, hidden to the outsider, but found in the journals and records of hospitals and thousands of private doctors, then we would see some terrible results which clearly would indicate that the estimated half a million alcoholics of our country by no means can be considered coming from just one certain· group of our society. It is true that alcoholism generally leads its victims to the slums, but we must not overlook the thousands, living useless lives, who suffer and die before they ever get to skid row.

"Pastor Erik Edin, now the director of Lewi Pethrus' Foundation for Philanthropic Ministry, came to my rescue; he is an energetic and truly Christian man whom many can thank for their conversion and salvation. May God give him strength, and may men and authorities give the foundation he serves resources to continue to expand this rescue ministry which has produced such wonderful results.

"Pastor Edin, whom I did not know at that time, had heard of my situation through one of my former employees and was given my address by a nursing home, where I had spent some time. He came to me, read the Bible and explained the wonderful truths concerning Christ's death and atonement. He did this in such a lucid and convincing way that I realized that even I was included, if I was willing to believe and receive this simple truth.

"Erik Edin did not limit his ministry to words and explanations only. Within a few days he had arranged a job for me, and he followed up my budding new life with love and thoughtfulness, with leniency and patience so that I really felt I had his support. His loving and altogether unselfish action gave me a tremendous confidence in Christianity and broke down any scepticism I had harbored and laid the foundation for a strong conviction that Christian action is essential if we want to bring people to faith in God.

"Saved and happy, I had success in my new employment, and when Lewi Pethrus' Foundation started the rehabilitation industries for alcoholics I was invited to head up this work. With personal and inside experience of alcoholism I am now daily working with rehabilitation of people, who on a Christian basis want to begin a new and useful life, and I find this a most fascinating task. To spend my strength and use my experience in so meaningful a mission has actually been therapy to my own necessary self-esteem.

"Today I know an inward peace and harmony which I never had in my earlier life. I have accepted and in my heart and mind received Christ's atonement by which I experience God as a reality. God is no longer just hearsay — something I would be embarrassed to talk about.

"God is a reality in our life and for all eternity, regardless of what quasi-scientists and other people may say. If they want to silence their inner anxiety for themselves and their children with all kinds of excuses and explanations, they are to be pitied, and it is the task of all believers to show them the way to Jesus Christ, the sinless One, who died on the cross bearing the sin and transgression of the world upon Himself in order that we and coming generations, as long as God decrees, may experience reconciliation and peace with God at the cross through faith in Jesus, and that in all our life and action He may be our great example."

The following personal accounts are rendered by people who by doctors were termed incurable alcoholics but who were rescued through the ministry of the foundation. We know them well and can guarantee their authenticity.

Eric Olov Pettersson tells the following story:

"At the age of seventeen I left my hometown and enlisted in the armed forces. There I began to be more intimate with liquor than before. If I had only known the terrible consequences of these so innocently appearing visits to the taverns!

"As a young man I was married, but the liquor habit was to bring disaster. Everything seemed to tumble down. My wife lost her patience and left me. I was altogether a victim of alcohol.

"I had to admit to myself that I was an alcoholic, a human wreck in the slums of the city jungle.

"Of course, doctors and temperance authorities did everything they could. I cannot number the times I have been in various hospitals and institutions — I gave up keeping a count of them.

"My first delirium tremens I experienced in 1955. Delirium tremens — no one who has not personally experienced it can fully realize what it is. An indescribable anguish, the room teeming with snakes, the ceiling coming down, the walls closing in, the rib cage squeezed by a slimy monster which looks straight into the brain with its only eye which burns like a welder's torch all the way into the very soul. One begins to choke . . .

"There are alcoholics, and not so few of them, who have died after one or two such experiences.

"Then I received my doom: You are incurable, you will be an alcoholic as long as you live.

"My first delirium was followed by two more, admittedly not quite as violent as the first one, and I was probably about to have my fourth one, when I met Jesus, and He saved me.

"After a long time of drinking in a city near Stockholm, when I had had nothing but the cheapest alcohol for both food and drink, I lay on the ground in a woods outside the city. My mind muddled by the poison, I was possessed with a determination to commit suicide. I had reached bottom now! Then suddenly one of my former drinking cronies came and found me. He had been saved and testified of how Jesus is able to deliver the slaves of sin.

"He was at that time in a home, Strandgarden, operated by Lewi Pethrus' Foundation for Philanthropic Ministry. A spark of hope was ignited. Maybe there was salvation for me also? Yes, thank God, through Jesus Christ — that which was impossible with men God did!

"I can never forget that day. It was on July 31, 1960. After a phone call to the director of the foundation I was told I could come there.

"And it was there I experienced the turning point in my life. The Word reached my bleeding heart, and I met Jesus Christ as my Savior.

"There were still days of battle and agony; I had so many things to straighten out, and this led to great problems. How could I solve them? But even in that situation the Word was a tremendous help. In the sixth chapter of Matthew, verse thirty three we read: 'Seek ye first the kingdom of God, and his righteousness; and all these things shall be added unto you.'

"I have indeed, experienced that God is faithful.

"After some months I buried the old life through baptism in water and was added to the church. I want to stress how much the church has meant to me. The wonderful fellowship with God's people cannot be described. So much love I have truly never met before in my life. That I find myself in the faith after these nine years since I was saved, I attribute to a great extent to the fact that there have been people who have been willing to place confidence in me. Anyone can understand that it can take a long time to regain the confidence of relatives, employers, and authorities, if one for decades has wasted one's life in the marshlands of alcoholism.

"After about half a year at Strandgarden, Rev. Edin spoke to me about a job as a custodian that he could offer me. I was overwhelmed!

"The apostle Paul says: 'I . . . who was before a blasphemer, and a persecutor and injurious' (I Tim. 1:13). Personally I diagnosed my former life in the following words: 'I was an alcoholic, a misfit, a social leper, and a parasite on society'—and to me this confidence was extended?

"From the beginning not too hard assignments were given me, but as time went by more and more responsibility was given to me.

"My nervous system was completely wrecked. My hands shook so badly that they almost had to feed me when I first came to Strandgarden.

"The job I was offered at Strandgarden was at times quite emotionally demanding. But it was remarkable to see how little by little I became more and more balanced. There were those who felt I was not emotionally fit to hold this position. And I can certainly understand them, especially those who had seen me when I first arrived at Strandgarden.

"In 1965 the foundation began a rehabilitation ministry in Jarbo, where some industries were opened. In 1966 I was placed there and given the responsibility for the dormitories. I have also found a wife who helps me and gives me moral support.

"The former slave of alcohol, whose shabby clothes had to be burned, and in whose pockets only a penny could be found, has been transformed by the Gospel and has become a useful citizen in our society.

"GIVE GOD THE GLORY!"

And now the far-traveling jazz musician Stig Gillberg shares with us his testimony of deliverance from a difficult case of alcoholism of many years' standing.

" 'Never did I know that life could be so full of joy, happiness and peace' — thus sings a well-known singing evangelist.

"This is no exaggeration. I was bound by sin and vices in such a way that for long seasons I felt anguish and despair night and day. When I rediscovered my childhood faith in Jesus Christ I found the way to a well ever-flowing with joy and peace. Difficult moments I have experienced both earlier and now — and who has not? But how wonderful that a Scripture, or just the thought of what Jesus did for us on Calvary or of God's mercy, can shatter the darkest thoughts in a matter of minutes.

"My dear parents, who were true believers, did their best trying to lead me onto the Christian road, but as a teenager I was foolish enough to listen more to my friends and to people with an altogether different philosophy of life. I became a great admirer of the jazz of the 50's, and I played in a number of bands both at home and abroad.

"This kind of life, however, never did give me real satisfaction. While still very young, I began to do more than just take a few social drinks. In fact, at 25 I was already an alcoholic. I sought help from doctors and from the temperance board. But this was only temporary relief. Soon I was back to my great problems again.

"Thank God, however, I had a number of people praying for me, and God heard their prayers. One day I realized that my problems basically were spiritual ones. Then I cried to Jesus for help, and He set me free first of all from my warped and negative attitude toward everything and everybody. Then Jesus continued to break the fetters, one after another — liquor, tobacco, and foul language, a critical spirit, bitterness, envy, etc. Often we still find that the devil tries to put us under similar bondage again, but then we have to go back to the Cross.

"I have seen many brothers experience the same freedom during the years I have been associated with the Lewi Pethrus' Foundation, for it was at the home of this foundation, in Strandgarden, where I began to take my first few wobbly steps of faith. Now I am the custodian of this home and have daily fellowship with brethren who have started to follow the same wonderful way.

"My desire is to continue to give my time and interest to this ministry so richly blessed of God."

**Henry Gustavsson,** who heads up the clothing department of the foundation, is also a former alcoholic and drug addict who was miraculously saved. He writes:

" 'For the Son of man is come to seek and to save that which was lost' (Luke 19:10).

"Seven years ago, when I came to Strandgarden, I was humanly speaking a hopeless case. I was completely ruined by abuse of drugs and alcohol.

"In 1955 all government control of liquor was lifted. A couple of months after that I had lost my job, and within a year I had also lost my apartment. All hopes had been dashed, and everything I ever owned had been wrecked because of my desire for liquor. Everything was turned into liquor. Alcohol had become my master. I lived for one thing only — intoxication. I had to admit I was an alcoholic.

"Such was my situation when in 1955 I made contact with Rev. Edin. That year I received his book *I Was an Alcoholic*. I read it several times and thought that salvation might be the solution to my problem. But seven more years of the worst misery were to elapse before I made a decision.

"On March 29, 1962, I visited Rev. Edin's office. There I bowed in prayer, and my sins were forgiven. After that we went to Strandgarden. I did not then realize that Strandgarden was to be my home for four years. There I started a new life on a Christian foundation. I heard the Gospel, and I experienced the power of God unto salvation, and I found that there was enough grace for the chiefest of sinners.

"When I think of the alcoholic that was within me, I cannot help but believe that one cannot take the alcohol out of the alcoholic until he first has been delivered from alcoholism. Many tried to take away the alcohol from me — parents, brothers and sisters, doctors, temperance boards, temperance workers, social workers, employers, fellow workers — but no one was able. Personally I thought that if I could only get a job and an apartment I would sober up and be a better man. Then I got these, but within a few weeks I had created a new environment of alcoholism. If an alcoholic is to be cured he has to get something better, and that's what

I got at Strandgarden. There the Gospel was preached twice daily. When I received this Gospel, I was delivered from my desire for liquor. I received something better than alcohol — the Word of God.

"Strandgarden also became a real help in my material and temporal needs. God ministers to the whole person and wants to cure the entire man. I don't think God is looking at old sins, but that He is creating new men.

"Now I am working in the office of the Lewi Pethrus' Foundation in Stockholm, and there I have opportunity to testify to my old cronies that there is a way and a possibility to be free from the desire for alcohol. That way and that possibility is the Gospel of Jesus — He who came to save sinners.

"I thank God that there is a home like Strandgarden. There I found mercy and grace, and I was helped in the time of need."

The last personal testimony I want to share with my readers is that of a young lady, who in a wonderful and divine way was set free from a life in the deepest misery. Her deliverance came in the summer of 1969, and she is one of the many we meet in our ministry. I heard this testimony from Ann's own lips.

Ann is 25. She has been in prison three times. Her body has been punctured by needles from whose points drugs have been squeezed into her bloodstream.

She began taking pills when she was fifteen — and wanted more and more. Her body demanded more drugs — and her friends insisted she should take more, the friends she met on her way from school when she stopped in at the coffee shop.

She didn't have any place to go.

It was there it all started. And then it went from bad to worse — pills and hypos cost money.

Ann tried to pass bad checks — not very large amounts, but still a dishonest way of getting funds. She even was involved in some burglaries. Then she started to push drugs.

The road downhill was steep — her own road away from her sweet, beautiful, and pure early youth.

Ann could not continue her schooling. She could not even finish the last couple of semesters of high school. She dropped out.

She left her parents and her brothers. Sensible and intelligent thinking had no place in the frightening imaginary existence the drug abuse brought about.

Then she was put in prison and there gave birth to a son — a scrawny little creature whose blood was ruined because of the kind of life the young mother had lived. The doctors changed blood several times and saved the life of the little one.

Ann is now a happy young woman. She is free. Her time in prison was reduced to one third of the original sentence, "provided you stay out of trouble."

And it appears that young Ann will do just that, for she is completely delivered from the cravings for drugs.

She experienced this in a moment — in a twinkling of an eye.

It happened when Kathryn Kuhlman in the beginning of May 1969 spoke in the Frolunda Hall in Gothenburg. Ann tells about her deliverance in the following words:

"Miss Kuhlman asked if someone wanted to be delivered. She asked if there was a drug addict in the service; in fact, she said that there was such a person present. But I could not believe that she had me in mind. I only knew that I wanted to go forward. I did not understand what it meant to be saved; I thought this kind of thing happens to others — but not to me.

"I sat there on the very brink, jumped up and went forward. Words fail to describe what I experienced, but I felt I was free. I have begun a completely new life."

I asked Ann, "Were you completely delivered from your drug addiction?"

"Yes, completely," Ann replied. "I left the prison in November with my five-weeks-old baby, and I had had a very

- 134 -

difficult time during my stay in the prison. I had taken drugs for many years and had gone through withdrawal pains several times. The doctors had told me that I was a hopeless case, and that 'no doctor on earth can help you.'

"I know this now that no doctor could help me — but now I am free, completely free!"

Ann had not heard about Jesus in her home. She had never gone to Sunday school and never had any contact with Christians until she was put in jail.

A God-fearing woman, a financial consultant, visiting a pastor in Gothenburg happened to see some pictures of a young girl who was giving herself some shots of drugs with a hypodermic needle.

This was Ann.

The God-fearing woman was moved by Ann's condition. She managed to get her address, the prison where she was, and wrote to her. She wrote about Jesus who is able to save and to liberate us from all evil habits. Then she sent the book, *The Cross and the Switchblade*. Ann responded by writing.

The financial consultant looked up Ann when she was in the hospital to have her baby. Ann found a faithful friend in her. Such a friend she had not had since the day she left her parents' home.

"Now," Ann says, "I have found so many wonderful friends. I never knew that there were people like these. I had never had any contact with real Christians before. Now here in the Smyrna church, what wonderful friends I have found!"

Ann has had more answers to prayer than the instantaneous deliverance — in a moment — from her drug addiction and the slavery of sin. And now she has contact with her parents and her two brothers, she tells me.

"My boy was healed from high fever, when I requested prayer for him.

"And when after an aptitude test I was accepted as a student in a typing class, I wanted to take the class but was without funds. The tuition for that particular class was $200.

I talked to my mother on the phone about my problem, then I prayed to God for help, and the following morning while I was again speaking to mother, the mailman came and delivered a letter with a $100 scholarship.

"And now my boy's blood count is much better. God answers prayer."

Ann is now temporarily employed in a home for girls, and the doctor's wife says: "She is fantastically positive, she radiates happiness. That which happened to her was a great miracle."

These few and brief statements are but a small part of the powerful testimony which multitudes of former alcoholics and drug addicts in our midst could share with us. These accounts speak eloquently of the power of the Gospel when it is experienced in its fullness.

*VIII*

# Jesus' View Of Man

## AS THE GUIDELINE OF THE CHURCH

The many-sided mission of living Christianity in the world could be summarized in one single task, namely, to rescue men and women from a life without God to a life in fellowship with Him.

The church, in other words, exists for the purpose of making real the view that Jesus has had of man, and then effecting a ministry appropriate to this view. His concept of man is clearly depicted in the New Testament and is different from that of his contemporaries. There is a danger that the Christian church of today has lost the picture of man which Jesus painted in such a colorful way in His life and ministry.

There are three features in particular in this view of man which deserve to be stressed. First of all He considered man as an individual. The collectivism which controlled the religious thinking at the time of Christ had no place in His view of man. He was no slave under the multitude nor under its authority. Multitudes gathered around Him, but even then He took an interest in individuals. He always managed to find someone in the throng with a particular need. That one interested Him especially, and to him or her He turned His attention.

Some of the most wonderful statements the Gospels have preserved were made to individual persons. Nicodemus, the woman at the well, and blind Bartimaeus are examples of people in distress to whom He addressed His wonderful thoughts and words.

In the cycle of parables concerning lost man which Luke records in the 15th chapter of his Gospel, Jesus underscores the value of a single person and of his salvation. The Christian church of today in many places has fallen victim to a collectivism which endangers the view Jesus had of man. To win **one person** to God in our day is no particular recommendation for an evangelist or a missionary. No, they should be able to report that hundreds or thousands have been found before it will release any great enthusiasm among today's friends of the Good Shepherd. We never know, however, how many of these conversions reported in present-day public-relations articles heaven actually rejoices over.

It is apparently the person who wins one by one that Jesus desires to encourage. He heavily underlines the value of the individual: "And when he [the shepherd] cometh home, he calleth together his friends and neighbours, saying unto them, Rejoice with me; for I have found my sheep which was lost. I say unto you, that likewise joy shall be in heaven over **ONE** sinner that repenteth, more than over ninety and nine just persons, which need no repentance" (Luke 15:6, 7).

He underlines individualism in this context by speaking of **ONE** single sinner.

There is a danger that the individual will disappear in a movement such as Christianity. It appears, namely, with the collective thought of the church and with the idea of a movement. To warn us against this danger, Christ has given us a clear and thought-provoking teaching. This individualistic view pervades also His teaching about God's protective care of the believers. He speaks of how not even a sparrow falls to the ground without His will. The smallest details in the lives of those who believe in Him are noted in His store of knowledge. In this context He uses an expression which may seem to be an exaggeration, namely, that the very hairs on their heads are numbered. The church also exists for the sake of the individual. Notice that the only time Jesus speaks of the local church, He is concerned about the individual, the salvation of the individual.

There are those who maintain that the church exists only for members who live a victorious life. One pictures the church as an exhibition of splendid specimens of Christians which the world can view with admiration. This is not the picture Jesus draws.

The church in His view looks more like a sculptor's shop into which blocks of stone have been brought from "the rock from when they were hewn." No one but Jesus can in these recognize an image which will gain entrance into the heavenly exhibition hall. Much of the old environment, which must be cut away with the Master's chisel, before the work is finished, comes into the sculptor's shop. We may also think of that shop as the place where the stones are prepared to be fitted into the divine temple.

These stones may be thought of as living stones (I Pet. 2:5 RSV) which are very sensitive to chisel and hammer which they must endure. Therefore, if they sin, they are to be treated with the pity and care Jesus describes in such detail. If someone sins he should first of all be approached in a personal way by the person who first finds out about it. Let us read what Jesus says:

"Moreover if thy brother shall trespass against thee, go and tell him his fault between thee and him alone: if he shall hear thee, thou has gained thy brother. But if he will not hear thee, then take with thee one or two more, that in the mouth of two or three witnesses every word may be established. And if he shall neglect to hear them, tell it unto the church: but if he neglect to hear the church, let him be unto thee as an heathen man and a publican" (Matt. 18:15-17).

Here again the Lord is concerned about the individual. The church must never yield to this devastating collectivism where the individual drowns in the big crowd. On the other hand, the membership roll must not be considered to the extent that one hesitates to exercise church discipline by separating from the church those who want to live in sin.

The primary purpose of the church, however, is not church

discipline but rather care for the members. It is the church's great mission to save souls, not just by winning them to Jesus and to the church, but to keep saving them when necessary since they have become a part of the church.

Another consideration is that Jesus includes the whole of man in his view of man. God had in the law of Moses shown that His care for man touched all his needs. The Israelite covenant in the days of Jesus had lost this total picture of God's care and had confined it to just the spiritual.

Present-day Christianity is characterized by the same one-sidedness. One cleaves man in two. The spiritual part is turned over to the church. The other part, namely man's body and his material life, the church turns over to the world. But Jesus took an interest in man's physical needs as well as in his spiritual needs. His salvation included man's body. This is why the healing of the sick was a part of His ministry.

Neither did He exclude man's need of daily bread from His concern. He made sure that the people got something to eat when they had remained with Him so long that they became hungry. He even employed His supernatural power to provide the bread that was needed.

One of the most touching events in the life of Jesus is when after His resurrection He shows His concern about the physical needs of the disciples. During the forty days between the resurrection of Jesus and His ascension, the disciples began to worry about their daily bread. The treasurer of the little band of disciples had committed suicide, and there was no support for them and their families. One of those days Peter said: "I go fishing." This was his old trade. Some have interpreted this return to the old trade on the part of the disciples as an expression of their unbelief. But, I am sure, this was not the case. Then Jesus would not have helped them with their fishing as He did. It shows rather that in the midst of supernatural experiences they kept their feet on the ground. They realized that they were just plain people who needed to make their living in a regular way.

While they were toiling, however, in order to provide for themselves and their families, Jesus came to them. He came in a moment when even their tradesmanship was severely tried. Compelled by real needs, they had gone fishing and had totally failed and were ready to go ashore with empty boats. Then Jesus came. It was the risen Christ who presented Himself.

In the midst of their battle for their daily bread, they saw Jesus standing on the shore. Presently He spoke to them. One might have expected that His inquiry would be concerned about their spiritual life, but not so; His question was concerning their daily bread, for He says, "Children, have ye any meat?"

When they in response explain their failure, He helps them catch a great draught which filled their needs for rent and food for some time. But this was not all. When the disciples landed, they noticed a fire which Jesus had started, and on it He was preparing breakfast for them. He asked for some of the fish which they had caught, and then He invited them: "Come and dine!"

This illustrates how human the risen Savior is and His great concern for man's human needs. He includes the whole man. It is this attitude that He wants His church to have toward the physical need of man. None of the concerns of man must be considered outside the care of the church.

Christ also had a message for the cities; He reprimanded them when they as communities had failed to listen to Him. His view of man included the whole man – and even the social conditions in the community.


## JESUS GIVES PRIORITY TO THE PRODIGAL

Jesus presents another side of His view of man which needs special attention in our days. He gives to the lost, and most hopeless, priority before the righteous who need no repentance. This is an attitude no one else up to that time had advanced in the history of man.

Jesus sees the man. Neither spiritual, moral nor social conditions were particularly significant in His evaluation of the human being. He could meet man in the form of a sinful woman, or in the person of Nicodemus, or the rich young ruler. The outward appearance made no impression upon Him, and He paid no attention to it. To Him they were all just people, and it was their value as such which He saw, and as such He viewed and treated them.

Without hesitation we can say that Jesus is the One who discovered and revealed man. During the course of history, man, the crown of creation, has been buried under prejudices based on riches, learning, social status, race, and color of skin. Out of all this debris Jesus has brought forth the precious pearl that man is in His sight. With the preaching of Christ and His breaking down of all walls of segregation between people, the dignity of man has been restored. Even men and movements which have not been Christian, but have proclaimed the dignity of man, originally received this view from Christianity.

With this starting point of the intrinsic value of man, Jesus gives priority to the Prodigal. In the parables of the lost sheep, the lost coin, and the prodigal son, this principle is presented in a colorful way. In conjunction with man's restoration to fellowship with God, Jesus gives priority to the worst. It is easy to see the reason for this.

All have gone astray. All need to be restored to a right relationship with God. The lost sheep needs to be brought back to the care of the Shepherd. The lost coin must be returned to the owner. The lost son must get back to the Father with whom he has his real home.

The outward scale of values which separates people from one another is of no importance when it comes to man's relationship to God. This is why salvation is placed on the level where the worst one is found. He realizes his need of help; and irrespective of the level on which a person may think he is, it is necessary for him to descend from his illusionary heights to the level where salvation is offered. It can be received only by him who sees himself as a lost sinner.

The apostle Paul was according to the law an irreproachable man; but when he summarized everything he had done against God and His cause, he ended up realizing that he was chief among sinners. In this way the first must become the last in order to obtain salvation. Everyone must descend to the level where priority is offered to the worst ones. There man finds that "where sin abounded, grace did much more abound" (Rom. 5:20).

It was this view of man which the Jewish theocracy had lost. There was no mercy for the sinner. Only the morally good and strong had any possibility to have fellowship with God. The grace and mercy which had found an expression in the law of Moses had disappeared from their theology, and only the few chosen ones who had managed to get into the party of the Pharisees could have any share in the fellowship with the living God.

We have the Pharisees' view of man also in our Christian work today, namely, he who belongs to a Christian church, and especially the type of church of which I am a member, enjoys the favor of God. But the large throng which lives without God is outside of God's love and care. The children of God are loved by Him, but upon the rest of the world the wrath of God is resting. This, however, is not the view of man which Jesus espoused.

In His conversation with Nicodemus, He treated this question. He relates how "Moses lifted up the serpent in the wilderness, even so must the Son of man be lifted up: That whosoever believeth in him should not perish, but have eternal life." Then He adds: "For God so loved **the world**, that he gave his only begotten Son, that whosoever believeth in him should not perish, but have everlasting life" (John 3:14-16).

Nicodemus thought that God loved Israel only, but Christ proclaims that God loves the world.

It is this world of men, of lost individuals, which Jesus has brought into focus. The commission of the church is to save this world.

Only as the church keeps in mind this view of man which Jesus has given us can she fulfill her mission.

Like the erring sheep was helpless, defenseless, without sense of orientation, unable without assistance to find the way back to the shepherd, so the sinner is helpless in his lost condition. That is why we must seek him and rescue him.

Like the missing coin represented a value which had been lost, so the sinner is a value which must be sought and found and then be invested in the kingdom of God.

Like the prodigal son tried the father's love through disobedience, the wasting of his inheritance, and the disgrace he brought upon the father's name and above all, his cruel way of hurting the father's feelings, so the sinner has made himself unworthy of God's love and care. Still Jesus assures us that God's love for the world remains just as warm. The father of the parable saw the returning son afar off, made arrangements to have garments, shoes, and a ring ready for the boy, ran to meet him, and in great tenderness and love reunited him with the father's home. Even so the love of God to the sinner is changeless and without the least shadow of upbraiding.

It is true of many that they have lost sight of the sinner as an individual. They are interested in the work of God, and the sinner has become just a detail in the routine. Others have totally put aside evangelization and concentrate their interest on Christian education. Then there are some who continue to conduct revival meetings, but only because it belongs to the ministry. One is not really concerned about the sinner, but one is interested in gaining new members for the church. It is considered a merit to see an increase in the membership, and it gives added prestige to those who can report many conversions in their revival meetings. To some the sermons and the general appearance of the activities of the church dominate their interest, and the distress and predicament of the sinner is of little concern. The intrinsic value of the sinner, and the thought of making a contribution which would cause heaven to rejoice receives altogether too little attention in our churches today.

It has been proven that the church which purposes to see sinners saved will enjoy the blessing of God upon its ministry in a special way. Some have asked how churches which in many ways do not function according to the pattern in the New Testament still have success and growth, while other churches which may be ever so scriptural in their doctrine and practices make no progress whatever. My experience has taught me that love for sinners and activity for their salvation means more to God than orthodoxy. God so loved the world that He gave His Son for the salvation of the world; and it was for the salvation of the sinner Jesus left heaven and glory, made Himself one with man and gave His life for the reconciliation of the world.

It was His view of man and His high evaluation of man which caused Him to give Himself for the salvation of the human race. The church has been commissioned to fulfill this ministry of saving souls. It is, therefore, the church's responsibility to acquire the view that Jesus had of man and then, gripped by this lofty view, to win the world for God.

# IX

# Liberty - Life's Loftiest Longing

## CHRIST – OUR CREED

## CHRIST – OUR CONFESSION

The Christian creed from the beginning was confined to the Person of Christ. He said: "Whosoever therefore shall confess me before men, him will I confess also before my Father which is in heaven" (Matt. 10:32).

The task of the disciples was to bear witness of the Person of Christ. We can readily see this in the fragments we have of their sermons. Peter's sermons on the Day of Pentecost and in Cornelius' house were concentrated around the Person and work of Christ. In the same manner Paul's preaching was very much Christocentric. Philip's ministry in Samaria is described as an example of how the scattered members of the Jerusalem church continued their proclamation, and it is · recorded about him that "Philip went down to the city of Samaria, and preached Christ unto them" (Acts 8:5).

When we nowadays speak of a creed we have in mind an enumeration of points of doctrine as understood and accepted by churches and denominations. The preaching has therefore often become a proclamation of various doctrines rather than teaching concerning the Person of Christ. One has even gone so far as to advance certain doctrines as the basis of salvation.

In Christ the whole of the divine truth is concentrated. He says: "I am the way, the truth, and the life."

One of C. H. Spurgeon's biographers says that this great

preacher's theology was summed up in Christ. Spurgeon's theology could be likened to a mine in which he dug for the divine truth as revealed in the Holy Scriptures. Out of it he continually brought new treasures with which his listeners were enriched.

By accepting Christ as our creed we have come to possess the truth which is in Christ. He who owns a mine is owner not only of the treasures which have been taken out but also everything that is left. In like manner we can be blessed by truth which we have not yet understood nor been able to assimilate.

Salvation is not based on the fact that we accept or believe in certain doctrines. One Monday morning I received a phone call from a man who had listened to my preaching on Sunday. He said that he wanted to talk to me before he went to work that morning. He came to see me, and it was evident that he was greatly troubled about his soul's salvation. But he said that there was one thing which troubled him — he could not believe in eternal punishment.

I assured him that there is nothing which would tie his salvation to such a belief. It is faith in Jesus which saves — not acceptance of or belief in certain doctrines. The man believed in Jesus and received Him as his Savior and went away relieved after our visit together.

In this context, Paul's words to the jailer at Philippi can serve as a dependable guide. When the question was raised: "Sirs, what must I do to be saved?" the apostle Paul responded, "Believe on the Lord Jesus Christ, and thou shalt be saved, and thy house" (Acts 16:30,31). It is faith in Jesus which saves and not believing in the doctrines about Him.

The Bible does not present any systematic theology. Neither Christ nor the apostles developed anything like that. At times such a document has been drawn up, and it has only served to confirm the divisions among God's people. It has more often been used as a weapon against others than as a life buoy for the salvation of our fellowmen.

# TOWARD THE WHOLE TRUTH

How often human limitations have put their stamp on an event as divine and wonderful as a spiritual revival. It has often happened because the person who more than others spoke for the revival thereby made his imprint on the spiritual movement because he kept it within the frame of his own spiritual limitations. Whatever might have been revealed to this person of the divine truth in the Scriptures has set the course of the movement for the future. Then if this is expressed in a confession of faith, it will only hasten the hardening and decline of the revival.

When through the Reformation the truth concerning justification by faith came alive, Christ was, of course, glorified. Christ's atonement came into the very center of preaching and of believing. When this condition changed and the splendor of the personal Christ diminished, confessions of faith and tenets about the doctrine of atonement began to develop. And since then the battle about these various teachings has actually hidden the Atoned Himself.

It has been the same way with other biblical truths. Those who received them and experienced the blessing of appropriating them have built confessions around them. Unintentionally, no doubt, there is created a sort of monopoly regarding the truth and the revival movement. One person may have proclaimed himself a special representative of this truth which is called distinctive of the movement.

In such a way one actually detaches the biblical truth from its context. This is, of course, detrimental to the person who confines himself to one particular truth. Then it is a detriment to the Christian message and God's cause in general.

The various truths in the Scriptures are in the spiritual world what the natural resources are in the plant world. Suppose a farmer would do what some believing theologians have done with Christianity. How would it turn out if he would say: "I consider the sun a spring of life for all vegetation, therefore I am all for the sun. I will preach it, and we will start a movement which in a more effective way than has been done before will stress the importance of the sun for the life of the plants."

Then someone else says: "I consider rain and irrigation the most important. I hold that this side of teaching has been stressed altogether too little, and therefore I will start a movement which will emphasize this need and do away with this deficiency." In similar fashion other farmers acted. One chose the fertility of the soil and had the fertilizing as his specialty, while another built up an interest in the seed and its growing power. Each one stressed his side at the expense of the others. The worst that could happen would be that they practiced what they taught. One permitted his crops to have sunlight but very little of other needs; another gave his fields water only, etc.

Anything so absurd would even be hard to imagine among agriculturists, that's for sure! And if anyone would dare make an attempt at this, he would soon be taken out of his delusion and would return to the prudent many-sidedness with which the Creator has endowed nature.

But some theologians do not hesitate to take apart the system of providing for the spiritual life which God has instituted in order that the spiritual life may grow and develop. God's church, His universal ecclesia, must be satisfied with being separated from divine resources according to what the creeds of the doctrinal fathers and the denominations may prescribe. Instead of permitting the whole divine truth, with its many nutritious ingredients to flow to the Christian multitude, they give it a limited fare, a kind of a religious diet which they call sound doctrine. And in an arbitrary way spiritual resources are rationed, although these are provided in just as abundant measure as those who fill the immense storehouse of nature.

It is tragic that men with their limited light in the Holy Scriptures will assume as delicate a task as to compose a Christian creed. This is why we have so many creeds. None has included the whole truth. Consequently, a little later someone else comes along who sees the truth which an earlier generation did not see. Another creed is formulated, a fence which separates the one group of Christians from the other.

If a person would arise with a perfect light and insight in the Word he might have reason to try to extract from the Scriptures all the truths and arrange them in a systematic way. It might have the advantage of making it easier to survey these truths, and easier to locate them. The trouble is, however, that there is no person who has a perfect understanding of the Scriptures and there never will be! The apostle Paul settled this: "For we know in part, and we prophesy in part. But when that which is perfect is come, then that which is in part shall be done away" (I Cor. 13:9, 10).

Since no one has a perfect light on the Word of God, no one ought to build a creed based on the Bible, and in so doing claim to clarify its contents.

One of the sad consequences of these creeds and confessions is that they hinder the people of God from progressing and experiencing growth in biblical truth, for with the creed one has already determined how far one can go. The truths one has built the creed around in that way become a hindrance which stunts the believer's progress.

Jesus said to His disciples before He left them that the Holy Spirit when He came would lead them into all truth. Jesus had in mind a great deal of saving truth. The disciples were not mature enough to receive everything that Jesus wanted to share. But they matured through the light of the Spirit and through new experiences. They certainly progressed in truth, which is evidenced in the account of their development. In spite of their privileged position and in spite of their development in truth they did not give us any systematic theology. What they did give us was their experience and their view of the truth which had been revealed to them.

The writer of Hebrews deals sharply with those who do

not grow in the divine truth. He admonished his readers to leave the first "principles of the doctrine" (Heb. 6:1). Most of those who have undertaken to write creeds, however, have remained around these first "principles of the doctrine" and some never proceeded any further.

A right attitude on this point creates humility and a hunger in the believer. Instead of imagining that he has the whole divine truth he realizes how little of it has been grasped. He experiences the poverty in spirit which awareness of ignorance creates. It is this kind of poverty Jesus lauds and says that it is different from other poverty in that it gives blessedness. With this approach one remains a seeker all through life, seeking more divine light and greater understanding of spiritual realities. One sees on the divine map of truth large white areas, and one hastens toward these in order to explore them.

## PERSONAL SOUL-WINNING

When Jesus assures the church that the gates of hell shall not prevail against her, He indicates also the basis for this victory: "Upon this rock I will build my church; and the gates of hell shall not prevail against it" (Matt. 16:18).

For thousands of years the meaning of these words of Jesus has been discussed.

The apostle Paul has formulated this side of the church's ministry in a clear and unmistakable way: "According to the grace of God which is given unto me, as a wise masterbuilder, I have laid the foundation [in Corinth], and another buildeth thereon. But let every man take heed how he buildeth thereupon. For other foundation can no man lay than that is laid, which is Jesus Christ"(I Cor. 3:10, 11).

Jesus asked His disciples: "Whom do men say that I the Son of man am?" In reply Peter answered: "Thou art the Christ, the Son of the living God." Then Jesus responded:

"Blessed art thou, Simon Bar-jona: for flesh and blood hath not revealed it unto thee, but my Father which is in heaven. And I say also unto thee, That thou art Peter, and upon this rock I will build my church; and the gates of hell shall not prevail against it" (Matt. 16:13-18).

Jesus on this occasion was not speaking of the foundation of the church in its real meaning. He is speaking of the building of His church and the basis upon which He was to build. Jesus had before Him a person who had received a thorough revelation of Christ, and He foreknew the place this man would have in the founding of the church. He looked beyond his weaknesses and his defeat, wherein he even denied his Lord and Savior. Jesus saw that there was something pure, good, and faithful in the innermost being of this disciple. His gaze penetrated beyond the cross and the defeat of the disciples in conjunction with His passion, and He saw the day when the church, built upon the foundation of the atonement and the resurrection flooded by the light of the Holy Spirit, would be founded through the preaching of this disciple. At the time of the appearance of the church before the world, Peter was to take the place of prominence which Jesus here predicted.

It proved true that on the Day of Pentecost Peter was a rocklike man. Before the murderers of Christ and the enemies of the disciples he had courage to step out with the testimony of the crucified and risen Savior. When the door was to be opened for the gospel to the Gentile world, Peter again proved to be a rock. He knew of the prejudices within his own circle in the newly founded church at Jerusalem, but he did not hesitate to follow the heavenly vision and the call to go to the house of Cornelius with the Gospel message. In these instances we see a perfect fulfillment of what Jesus had predicted concerning this "rock man" and his mission as a builder of the church.

Peter, however, was no exception in any other way than that he was the one who with his testimony laid the foundation of the church in Jerusalem as well as in the Gentile world. It was upon him and his testimony about Jesus that the actual building was founded in both of these instances. It was really the preaching of the revelation of Christ that he had which caused the mighty miracle of salvation on the Day of Pentecost in Jerusalem as well as in the house of Cornelius. It was a man with a divine revelation of Jesus through whom the building of the church took place on both of the cited occasions.

In this same manner His church was to be continually built. If this way of building were employed, the gates of hell would not prevail against the church. What Jesus predicted about Peter was his importance for the early Christian church. This was fulfilled. What happened to Peter, however, has happened with all those who have received a divine revelation of Jesus. Around them the church has been built, just as on the Day of Pentecost in Jerusalem and later in the house of Cornelius. All we need to do is to quickly glance at the group of Christians whom we usually call the Reformers. It was the divine truth of Christ which set their hearts on fire, and it was this revelation made flesh in their "rock nature" which created the spiritual movements around them. They have been persons with an open mind for divine truth, and they had courage to stand up for their revelation in a hostile environment even if it would cost them their lives.

People with a divine revelation of Christ have the qualifications to build up the church of God. Their experience of Christ and the divine truth which is in Him lend quality to their testimony. It brings power and the kind of courage which is necessary in order to stand alone, and in the face of opposition step out with the Christian message. The revelation itself makes them the kind of "rock persons" such tasks require.

But Jesus did not only intend for these giants to build His church. The same principle according to which God works in these chosen instruments He will use in the building of the Christian church. He desires to reveal Himself in a personal way to the individual heart so that such a person's intellect, will and emotions will be gripped by the divine truth. Because of the fact that Christ has been made real, the believer's mind will be made steadfast so that he, regardless of circumstances, can boldly bear the testimony of Christ. Wherever this may take place, the church is being built as men and women are saved and added to the Christian number.

When during my visit to Brazil in 1967 I had an interview with the governor of Rio de Janeiro, I asked for his opinion about the secret of the tremendous success the Pentecostal revival enjoyed in that country. He mentioned several reasons, but he felt that especially the active witness of the individual members in their everyday life must be kept in mind. He said: "You can place a Pentecostal believer in a factory or in any kind of enterprise, and it won't be long before everyone at his place of employment will know that he is Pentecostal. He will immediately make known his Christian ideals, and he is ready to witness to anyone about his faith. He is also concerned about getting his neighbors under the influence of the church of which he is a member, and before long he will be surrounded by a little group whom he has won to the Lord through his personal influence and testimony."

When Jesus received the answer from Peter – in the situation earlier discussed – He was face to face with a common man of the people. Peter had come directly from his occupation as a fisherman. He probably still had the calluses in his rough hands from the time he pulled ropes and boats.

There was no human sidelight which disturbed the stream of light from the divine revelation which flooded his inner world. Without the contemporary psychology, theology, and rhetoric taught in the schools, he was standing there. Just ahead of him was also the great moment of temptation, when it would be revealed that Jesus did not judge him by human measures in predicting that he would be a rock. Jesus saw him, beyond the denial, restored and filled with the Spirit and with the courage which only clear spiritual insight can give. What James says about Elijah could also be applied to this disciple of Christ: He was a man "subject to the same passions as we are."

Actually he lacked the most important qualifications which he, humanly speaking, ought to have possessed. It is very possible, however, that it was the lack of these qualifications which fitted him for the great task he was entrusted with on the Day of Pentecost in Jerusalem and later in the house of Cornelius.

I could cite a number of examples of people whom I have met, and who have been just such as Jesus was able to build His church upon and around. I know young girls who were the only believers in an area; through a revolutionizing spiritual experience Jesus became real to their hearts, and thus they spontaneously became the cause of a church growing up around them.

One of my best friends, a post-office employee, upon his retirement felt led of the Lord to look up a place in Sweden where there was no Pentecostal work. There he settled down to win men and women to God. Before he finished his earthly course, he had the opportunity to win a large number for the Lord, set a church in order, build some churches, and greatly change the conditions in a whole area.

This is a question of personal soul-winning! The local church, campaigns, and various church activities all have their place, but there is nothing which can take the place of personal ministry. If a church is to succeed it must place its emphasis on the ministry of individual members. I was pastor of a church for 47 years, and I have seen it grow from about 30 members to about 6,500. The cause of this increase of membership I ascribe above all to the zeal and purposeful ministry of the individual members. I spoke often about our responsibility to win men and women for God and my listeners were willing to be persuaded.

I can never forget Sister Rahm. She was advanced in years, worked hard in a little bakery which she owned, and always attended our services. One Sunday night when I came down from the platform, I met her in one of the aisles of the church. She took hold of my arm and asked me to follow her into the prayer room to pray for someone who was seeking the Lord for salvation. After we had prayed and the inquirer had thanked God for the forgiveness of sin, Sister Rahm introduced her to me. She was a lady I knew. She had been a member of the church, but a few years earlier she had left the fellowship, and since then lived for the world. But now she had returned to the Lord and was beaming with joy. Then Sister Rahm explained:

"I was here in church this morning and heard pastor Pethrus speak about the distress of lost souls and the importance of winning them for God. I then happened to think of this friend who several years ago left our church. Right then and there during the morning service I decided to look her up and went directly from the service to her home. I was well-received, spent the whole day with her, and then we went together to the meeting – with this result." Her expression of praise was so abundant that it can hardly be described.

Wherever you may place a person who has Christ truly living in his heart, there will grow up around him a work of

God, a contribution to the universal church. It is on this rock Christ continually builds His church. On this basis the church of Christ will find that the gates of hell can never prevail against her.

## THE RENAISSANCE OF INDIVIDUALISM

Individualism in a certain moderation is one of the secrets of Christianity; it is the secret of the reality of the Christian experience. It is the secret of the building of character which is so typical of the Christian ethic.

Individualism is, in the final analysis, the secret weapon of Christianity in the battle against evil and in the efforts to win the world for Christ.

The moderation which Christian individualism maintains is the group – the church. The local church may be ever so small or large, but this is the limit of Christian collectivism.

Our time is the era of large alliances and organizations. One believes in the masses; the speaker, the church, the newspaper journalist, the author and the mass media – all seem to agree that nothing can be accomplished unless the masses can be reached. In all this "mass culture" not only the individual has disappeared but also the small group and the Christian church. Today denominations, movements, and ecumenism represent the Christians in a country – and the ultimate is triumph of collectivism over the Christian individual and the church.

In the secular world collectivism has for its goal that the state should take all initiative and be responsible for all production. In this manner the individual and the small group will disappear from our society. The communist countries constitute the final phase of this development. Then we have reached the very culmination of the human structure of society. What will come after that?

This is the problem we are facing in our days; it is a problem which demands a solution. The march of events will not come to a standstill just because the last few steps on this road of mass movements have been taken. Things will continue to happen. It will mean the collapse of our culture, or, if we prefer a milder expression, the retreat of a culture from its excesses back to normal and more human conditions.

The man of today, and especially the youth, must prepare themselves for this. Here it is important that one really know what it is all about lest one should become nothing but a chip on the gambling table of voracious collectivism. God does not begrudge any person the privilege of an individual life with all the blessing and happiness it brings.

While collectivism hollows the thought-life of the individual and makes him a parrot, he only needs to see to it that his opinions agree with the creed and program of the collective. He will not have an opportunity to express any opinion of his own. If the great collective castle built of cards would collapse, he has no personal program.

It is a comfortable existence where there is no need to wrestle with any problems. This is in harmony with the development of our times. Everything appeals to comfort. One can be as apathetic as one cares to be. One need only ride with the current. This is perhaps the least complicated and may be also the most economically rewarding life — but what a life! When it is all over, you have nothing but a shell — no personal content.

Christ founded His kingdom and the success of His cause upon individuals and small entities. It is Antichrist who in the last days will further his cause via the masses. But Christ moves in the opposite direction. He builds on the individual, whom He chooses and equips for His task. In this program He employs no larger collective than the local church — but never any organization of such into a mass movement.

He speaks of His church as the "little flock": "Fear not,

little flock; for it is your Father's good pleasure to give you the kingdom" (Luke 12:32). He never built His work on the masses. He knows how impossible it is to make it a fit instrument in God's hand.

When Christianity entered the world through Jesus of Nazareth, we notice that He came alone. For a season multitudes gathered about Him, but when He came to the great work of His life, namely to atone for the sin of the world, He was alone. No one stood by Him. It was demonstrated that what the Israel collective could not do for the world the Son of Man did alone. God placed the salvation of the human race in the hands of one person. How wonderful this is! Just imagine if He would have placed it in the hands of one or several churches. The Catholic church has maintained that they are the sole custodians of salvation. How fortunate it is that this is not so. Salvation is in the hands of Christ, and no church or council of churches is the custodian of the wonderful riches of salvation.

Christianity suffers a terrible loss when the individual's freedom and his place in Christian work is taken from him. The work of God is so great and the space so expansive that there is room for every individual to freely grow. He should have the right to take the initiative he is able to carry out. No church or leadership in any church can, according to the New Testament, hinder this. One of the reasons for little success and much stagnation in a church is often that individuals who could make a fruitbearing contribution have been hindered by an exaggerated collectivism.

The work of God with, and in, the individual characterizes the cause of Christ. It is to this end that the Christian experience aims. If we follow Him to His shop where he causes His tools to go through a process which will make them fitted for His work, we will be surprised at the personal treatment He will give. With care and love His eye is watching the forge where the material is made pliable, and then it follows the hammer as it forms the tools on the anvil for their task. There is no mass production here. It is strictly handcraft where each individual will bear the stamp of special, personal treatment.

## SPIRITUAL FREEDOM

Christianity began as a revival movement, and as long as it was just this it enjoyed great success. During the first century it occupied one country after another and one continent after another. Christianity's simple, unaffected, robust incarnation of Christ and His Spirit dealt a blow which neither material nor spiritual forces could resist. With the weight of an avalanche it made its way through the morass of Jewish doctrines, pagan philosophies, and idolatry, bringing the message of the Crucified.

Christianity has always shown the greatest strength and vitality and has been most expansive when it has maintained its original character of a revival movement. The local church must also be free and flexible if it is to be an instrument of continual revival. Then church and revival can have a mutual influence upon each other. The spirit of revival creates freedom in the church, and the church's flexibility and freedom are a condition for spiritual revival.

Christianity is life – spiritual life. If you place strong bands around that which is living there remain only two alternatives. Either the living will be choked to death or the life will break the bands and enable the new unhindered life to find its own way with possibilities for further growth and expansion. This is exactly what has happened in Christianity throughout the entire history of the church. Ever since the early church was wrapped in denominational systems, many bolted the organizations during the ever-recurring revivals.

One of the first mass bolts of this kind became known as Montanism. When the church through its organization, its dogmas, and its clergy had choked most of the spiritual life, the gifts of the Spirit and the spiritual ministry gifts were banned from the churches connected with the organized church.

Montanism was a great and powerful movement with outstanding men in its ranks, such as the prominent church father Tertullian. The aim of the movement was to return the church to its original place and to revive the exercise of the gifts of the Spirit and the spiritual ministry gifts. This revival has been compared and depicted as nothing but sheer mysticism. Of course, it possessed weaknesses like all movements where human action is involved. It is evident, however, that the tendency was correct. The reaction against the declension of the church and the positive aim to enrich the spiritual life, as in most revival movements, were brought forth by a crying need in that day.

In the steps of Montanism, countless revival movements have broken forth and shaken churches and denominations down to the very foundations. Every time a tide of spiritual life has rolled, this phenomenon has been repeated. One can observe a sort of a round and round motion of revivals and organizations. In this context we can establish some facts which should teach a lesson to those who have anything to do with spiritual work and ministry.

Isn't it remarkable that a church organization as such never is the bearer of a spiritual renewing or of a revival? Rather, the individuals or smaller groups within the denominations are the instruments in such movements. The aim has always been to reform or renew the church of which the leaders of the spiritual movements were members. This was also the intention at the time of the Reformation. The stated purpose was a reform within the church, but instead they bolted and established new churches.

Later when the Protestant churches became the objects of new revival movements the same procedure was repeated. The churches remained unchanged, and the spiritual movement which had for its goal a renewal of the already established work, was unable to effect any change within the church. Lest the new life-giving stream would be choked by the denominational system, it had to break through and find a new riverbed and the dissenter churches began.

It is also apparent that these spiritual life movements are a natural occurrence in the spiritual world. As the spring flood rises at a certain time of the year, and breaks forth, often with an irresistible force, so in the life of the Christian church there are times when the spiritual life storms ahead like a mighty flood. The spring flood is a product of existing conditions. Where it causes damage, it is because people have not adjusted to its existence nor taken proper precautions in view of various circumstances. The organizations which have been built up around the churches are too narrow and too small to contain the bountiful flows which a spiritual renewing brings. Such a movement, therefore, usually breaks and splits the denominations in its path.

Nevertheless, these spiritual life movements, again and again, have brought a new spiritual life into Christianity and many times changed life in general in our society.

It is inconsistent and actually inexplicable that these spiritual movements end up in the same denominationalism they once left. The most liberated and living movements find themselves in just a few years in organizations which are just as rigid and unmanageable as the denominational system they once departed from. In this way the circle is closed again and again; the circumvolution has been completed, and it is time for a new revival with the freedom such a movement always bears in its bosom.

When a spiritual movement through the decenniums has built up the instruments which are needed for spiritual work, and these then should be put to work by the new spiritual tide which comes, it is often barred by the organized collective and is forced to find another way. The already well-prepared tools for ministry may stand unfruitful for lack of spiritual life and enthusiasm while the bearers of the new revival must build up new instruments for their ministry. The loss in terms of time, manpower and financial resources this process entails, no one seems to be concerned about. Such an impractical and unwise procedure is hardly practiced in any other field of our society. It is only the large ecclesiastical collectives and their leaders who can afford such waste!

These devastating methods are primarily the result of the neglect to honor the freedom of the early Christian church. Without such freedom Christianity cannot remain a continual revival which it was meant to be.

It is a matter of priorities. The individuals today are seeking a greater role in the active life of the church.

The ecclesiastical structures will survive as they merge and seek to dominate and intimidate the individual. The present worldwide charismatic renewal is saying in loud and clear language the individual comes first. It is the two or three coming together in His name that will decide the course of the renewal.

There is a fresh strong breeze of His Spirit sweeping the world. God is the source and the revival will increase so that His glory will fill all the earth.

SUGGESTED INEXPENSIVE PAPERBACK BOOKS
WHEREVER PAPERBACKS ARE SOLD
OR USE ORDER FORM.

| | | |
|---|---|---|
| A NEW SONG—Boone | AA3 | $ .95 |
| AGLOW WITH THE SPIRIT—Frost | L326 | .95 |
| AMAZING SAINTS—Saint | L409 | 2.50 |
| AND FORBID NOT TO SPEAK—Ervin | L329 | .95 |
| AND SIGNS FOLLOWED—Price | P002 | 1.50 |
| ANGLES OF LIGHT?—Freeman | A506 | .95 |
| ANSWERS TO PRAISE—Carothers | L670 | 1.95 |
| ARMSTRONG ERROR—DeLoach | L317 | .95 |
| AS AT THE BEGINNING—Harper | L721 | .95 |
| BAPTISM IN THE SPIRIT—Schep | L343 | 1.50 |
| BAPTISM IN THE SPIRIT—BIBLICAL —Cockburn | 16F | .65 |
| BAPTISM OF FIRE—Harper | 8F | .60 |
| BAPTIZED IN ONE SPIRIT—Baker | 1F | .60 |
| BEN ISRAEL—Katz | A309 | .95 |
| BLACK TRACKS—Miles | A298 | .95 |
| BORN TO BURN—Wallace | A508 | .95 |
| CHALLENGING COUNTERFEIT—Gasson | L102 | .95 |
| COMING ALIVE—Buckingham | A501 | .95 |
| CONFESSIONS OF A HERETIC—Hunt | L31X | 2.50 |
| COUNSELOR TO COUNSELOR—Campbell | L335 | 1.50 |
| CRISIS AMERICA—Otis | AA1 | .95 |
| DAYSPRING—White | L334 | 1.95 |
| DISCOVERY (Booklet)—Frost | F71 | .50 |
| ERA OF THE SPIRIT—Williams | L322 | 1.95 |
| 15 STEPS OUT—Mumford | L106 | 1.50 |
| FROM THE BELLY OF THE WHALE—White | A318 | .95 |
| GATHERED FOR POWER—Pulkingham | AA4 | 2.50 |
| GOD BREAKS IN—Congdon | L313 | 1.95 |

| | | |
|---|---|---|
| GOD IS FOR THE EMOTIONALLY ILL —Guldseth | A507 | .95 |
| GOD'S GUERRILLAS—Wilson | A152 | .95 |
| GOD'S JUNKIE—Arguinzoni | A509 | .95 |
| GOD'S LIVING ROOM—Walker | A123 | .95 |
| GONE IS SHADOWS' CHILD—Foy | L337 | .95 |
| GRACE AND THE GLORY OF GOD —Benson/Jarman | L104 | .1.50 |
| HEALING ADVENTURE—White | L345 | 1.95 |
| HEALING LIGHT—Sanford | L726 | .95 |
| HEAR MY CONFESSION—Orsini | L341 | 1.00 |
| HEY GOD!—Foglio | P007 | 1.95 |
| HOLY SPIRIT AND YOU—Bennett | L324 | 2.50 |
| JESUS AND ISRAEL—Benson | A514 | .95 |
| JESUS PEOPLE ARE COMING—King | L340 | 1.95 |
| JESUS PEOPLE—Pederson | AA2 | .95 |
| LAYMAN'S GUIDE TO HOLY SPIRIT—Rea | L387 | 2.50 |
| LET THIS CHURCH DIE—Weaver | A520 | .95 |
| LIFE IN THE HOLY SPIRIT—Harper | 5F | .50 |
| LONELY NOW—Cruz | A510 | .95 |
| LORD OF THE VALLEYS—Bulle | L018 | 2.50 |
| LOST SHEPHERD—Sanford | L328 | .95 |
| MADE ALIVE—Price | P001 | 1.50 |
| MANIFEST VICTORY—Moseley | L724 | 2.50 |
| MIRACLES THROUGH PRAYER—Harrell | A518 | .95 |
| NICKY CRUZ GIVES THE FACTS ON DRUGS —Cruz | B70 | .50 |
| NINE O'CLOCK IN THE MORNING—Bennett | P555 | 2.50 |
| NONE CAN GUESS—Harper | L722 | 1.95 |
| OUT OF THIS WORLD—Fisher | A517 | .95 |
| OVERFLOWING LIFE—Frost | L327 | 1.75 |
| PATHWAY TO POWER—Davidson | L00X | 1.50 |
| PENTECOSTALS—Nichol | LH711 | 2.50 |
| PIONEERS OF REVIVAL—Clarke | L723 | .95 |

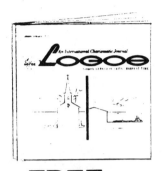

**FREE**
SAMPLE COPY
OF

# Logos

*An International Charismatic Journal*

Worldwide Coverage
Feature Articles
Book Reviews
Trends

**order blank on next page**

-------WHEREVER PAPERBACKS ARE SOLD OR USE THIS COUPON-------

WBS
Box 292, Plainfield, NJ 07061

## SEND INSPIRATIONAL BOOKS LISTED BELOW

| Title | Cat. No. | Price | |
|-------|----------|-------|---|
| _____ | _____ | _____ | ☐ Send Complete Catalog |
| _____ | _____ | _____ | |
| _____ | _____ | _____ | ☐ Free Sample copy of the LOGOS Journal |
| _____ | _____ | _____ | |

☐ 1 year subscription LOGOS Journal $3.00. Make payment to
WBS, Box 292, Plainfield, NJ 07061

Name _____

Street _____

City _____ State _____ Zip _____